**ANCHOR BOOKS**

EXPRESSIONS FOR A NEW CENTURY FROM SOUTHERN ENGLAND

Edited by

Neil Day

First published in Great Britain in 2000 by
ANCHOR BOOKS
Remus House,
Coltsfoot Drive,
Woodston,
Peterborough, PE2 9JX
Telephone (01733) 898102

All Rights Reserved

Copyright Contributors 2000

HB ISBN 1 85930 764 7
SB ISBN 1 85930 769 8

FOREWORD

Anchor Books is a small press, established in 1992, with the aim of promoting readable poetry to as wide an audience as possible. We see ourselves as a platform for new and established poets to build upon their talents and see their work in print for possibly the first time.

Each of the chosen poems has been specifically favoured from a large selection of entries sent. As always the editing proved to be a difficult task and as the editor, the final selection was mine.

Expressions For A New Century From Southern England is a unique collection of poetry and verse written in a variety of styles and themes, brought to us from many of today's modern and traditional writers, who reside in this area. The poems are easy to relate to and encouraging to read, offering engaging entertainment to their reader.

This delightful collection is sure to win your heart, making it a companion for life and perhaps even earning that favourite little spot upon your bookshelf.

Neil Day
Editor

CONTENTS

ANGEL LAND

There is another country,
far away yet near at hand,
close to all our yearning hearts,
a magic place, an Angel Land.

Wide rivers dance and twinkle
down to calm and rippling seas,
a soft warm breeze sighs gently
as it wanders through the trees.

Warm sunshine bathes your soul
with soft early evening light,
it's the best time of the day,
which never turns to night.

This wonderland seems empty,
but if you keep quiet and still,
you'll see the ghost-like shadows
of souls that roam at will.

All our dearly loved ones
have gone on to this fair place,
they wait for us to join them,
keep each of us a space.

Feel their presence round you
as you live your worldly years,
know that they watch and guide you,
sense them ease away your fears.

When your earthbound life is done
and it's time that you move on,
your travels will be guided
by those already gone.

Wendy Ray

GLORY DAYS

Where are the wheels of yesteryear
That turned a merry tune
Where are those heady summer days
That ended far too soon

Where are the shining silver knights
The dragons that they slayed
Where are the damsels in distress
The maidens that they saved

Where are the bows and arrows
The horses and the guns
Where is the false impression
Of how the west was won

Where is the buried treasure map
The pirates gave to me
Where is the skull and crossbones
That ruled a bygone sea

Where are the myths and legends
Enacted in my mind
They're lost within a childhood
That's now so hard to find

Ian Falconer

THE FATHER'S CREATION

Glorious world our Father's creation
Made by His hand as a haven for all
Given in love to each new generation
A wonderful gift from The Maker of all

Bountiful earth so graciously given
A place for all people to stand side by side
Striving together to reach the far heaven
There in the peace of God's love to abide

Father we thank you for all Your goodness
Constant, unchanging mercy and love
Call us to live within Your completeness
Safe evermore in Your mansions above

Barbara Scriven

BRACKLESHAM BAY

The wind swooped down from off the sea
With a hard solid hand
He tried his best to flatten me
Into a pattern on the sand.
He didn't succeed because I leaned
Full on his face, well-wrapped head
Buried in his beard.
His wild white hair flew horizontally
Make Fair Isle stitches clear and plain
Beaded with pearls of hail
Knitted with needles of rain.

The wind screamed up towards the Downs
And jumped on Trundle Hill
He whispered his way through Birdless Grove
Searching for Halnaker Mill.
He didn't succeed because he failed
And suddenly lost his power,
With almost the last of his frosty breath
He whined round Cackham Tower.
Wearily now he dived for the Nab
Skipped over Wight and away
Threading the Needles to drop like a stone
Tying a knot in the day.

Audrey G Willis

CHARITY SHOPS

I once bought a book about dolphins
From a High Street charity shop
Cost me nearly one pound fifty
Which caught me a bit on the hop.

In Oxfam I got a decanter
From which, perhaps, a general had sipped
I took it home and washed it
But alas I found it was chipped.

From Help the Aged I acquired my jeans
Tried 'em on for all to see
Put my hands in my pockets to test 'em
Cor blimey, I found 20p.

So well I remember that bird cage
Was complete except for a perch
But later that day I found one
On a shelf in Cancer Research.

The Animal Welfare was good
For an earthenware pot marked 'tea'
Cost me ten pence instead of a pound
Cos I swapped the labels you see.

Save the Children was busy that day
With twenty old dears or more
I paid for a Des O'Connor LP
Not knowing I'd owned it before.

Jenny Burton

STRIPPER

Slow hand clapping, we want action,
We've paid for the main attraction.
He strolls on stage, suave, uncaring,
The liquor makes us twice as daring.
We scream for him to 'Get 'em off,'
Sure as hell looks quite a toff.

Music thumping, he starts prancing,
Couldn't really call it dancing,
His clothes are dropping to the floor,
We stamp, we yell, we shout for more.
Gyrating hips so tantalising,
Now we're truly fantasizing.

> Eyes are goggling,
> Lord! We're boggling,
> Muscles rippling,
> We're still tippling,
> Buttocks gleaming,
> Is that me screaming?
> Give us more,
> Now what's the score?
> The thong's the thing,
> Just hear it ping,
> He's turning round,
> Don't make a sound,
> God! What a whopper,
> A real crowd stopper.

The party's over and we're returning,
To our homes but ever yearning,
To let our hair down, stamp and shout,
That's what it's really all about.

Helen Mitchelhill

DAISY

There is a canine heaven
Where doggies rest in peace
Chasing balls and eating chews
These pleasures never cease

Daisy Do, our furry friend is
Waiting there for us
She wants no tears or misery
No anguish or no fuss

She has no pains or aches or strains
She's happy now she's there
Her leaving was a bit too much
These feelings we can share

Daisy Do is at her best
She's chasing balls again
Running through the ditches
Thru sun and wind and rain

She keeps her eye on Toska
She keeps her eye on you
She's happy where she is right now
And hopes you're happy too

Pat Hennighan

SPOT THE DOG

As Spot the dog sits by my side
I thank my blessings for her by my side
She is so faithful, honest and true
She is so trusting, through and through
The only thing she loves to do
Is eat and sleep the whole day through

Keith Grover

GRAN'S HOUSE

When I was really very small
We shared Gran's house I do recall
Right beside the meadow there
We had such fun I do declare!
The house was very large inside
And lots of places where we could hide
A winding staircase up to the top
It's a house I never have forgot
So many memories lay there
With many friends living round about
Neighbours then were in and out
We imagined games that we would play
As money and toys were scarce in those days!
The old street lamp stood oh! So tall
But then of course, we were small
The greatest thrill would be Bonfire Night
Especially when we set it alight!
Times were very primitive then
So upon each other we did depend
No fancy clothes, or special shoes
We really had to make things do!
A darn in our sock was a familiar sight,
And the safety pin really stuck out!
In old Gran's house all the things I had seen
Were really true, they weren't a dream
Even now when I close my eyes
Those memories are all locked inside
I can't destroy them, they belong to me
In my memory album
Forever you'll be!

Patricia Holmes

THE OLD LADY

The old lady came from Bucklers Hard
Where men built Nelson's wooden walls,
A village where the life was hard
And people would not tolerate fools even gladly,
The old lady saved for weeks and months
To buy a new-fangled wireless set,
She listened to it every night
It only cost a few pounds net, but to her,
It was her world,
One evening wireless set went wrong
So come the morning she would phone
To Messrs Balls and Sons in town
The shop that she had bought it from,
Up to the phone box she did go
Shop's number written on a card,
A voice said 'Good morning
This is Balls from Lymington,'
And she said 'Oh yeah
Well this is asso from Bucklers Hard.'

Barry Lowe

AN ODE OF THANKS FOR MY KIND DOCTOR

It helps me to know that you'll listen,
It helps me to know that you'll care,
If only for seven short minutes
It helps me to know that you're there.

Without you I'm not sure I'd manage
Maybe fall by the wayside and die,
You give me the strength to keep going,
Renewing my effort to try.

I'm grateful for all that you're doing
For a rather sad person like me,
Your helpful support and bright smile
Much poorer without which I'd be.

I'm so lucky to have you to visit
When I'm feeling alone as I do,
So thank you dear, kind, caring doctor,
Thank you for just being you.

Beverley Arthur

FOREVER IN YOUR HEART

Do not be scared when I depart,
I'll stay forever inside of your heart.
I am the howling winds that blow,
I am the silent fall of snow.
I am the sound of pattering feet,
that awakens you from your deepest sleep.
I am the creaks you hear at night,
the sounds that give you such a fright.
I am the teardrop from your eye,
as you look at photos and begin to cry.
I am the birds up in the sky,
the plants, the grass and the trees so high.
You'll hear my heart inside the clock,
whenever you hear the tick, tick tock.
I am an angel up above,
looking over you with so much love.
So please don't cry now I've gone away,
cos in your heart and head I'll stay.

Sarah-Jayne Kelly

FLOWER

From a planted seed
soon to be freed
in all its glory
every flower has its story
such velvet petals
soft to the touch
unlike stinging nettles
that like to hurt so much
their carnival of abundance on show
oh how quick they like to grow
should they wither, or slowly die
they'll be replaced by you and I
wherever we are
they'll always be
together arranged so perfectly
they perfume any room
not shy to hide their beauty
when in full bloom
such power has any flower
an identity unto its own
never shall we forget the flower
for it often finds its way
into our *home*.

Lisa Read

A REFLECTION

The country lane's towered by an ancient beech tree.
Solid, imposing, with parasol verdant up there, free.
Many rural peasants must have broken bread and tarried there.
Many gay youngsters must have paid court and dallied there.
Did last century's squires come galloping by?

Now the same lane's neatly hedge trimmed, signposted,
Trees even grander, with grey limbs and body, still green head,
Nowadays no walkers will dawdle about or loiter there.
Lone ramblers will glance up but quickly move on from there,
For this century's fears come harassing by.

Susan Dawson

WHO WANTS TO BE A MILLIONAIRE?

Sometimes I sit and dream it's me,
Yes I've won the Lottery,
All the numbers on one line,
Six million will do, just fine.

Family and friends I have a few,
Will all want a share in it too,
Will come knocking I expect,
As I am presented with a cheque.

Thoughts are racing through my mind,
Now I've got the money, will I have time?
Seventy-nine, not old I hear you say,
Plastic surgery has come a long way.

Potions, lotions, creams and pills,
Am I really over the hill?
Money, money can't buy me time,
Only reduce my wrinkles and lines.

Alarm clock is ringing, as I wake up,
I couldn't really believe my luck,
It was all a dream now it's gone away,
And I am only thirty-three today.

Who wants to be a millionaire, not me,
I am happy being thirty-three.

Marie Mackinnon

EMPTY DREAMS

What happened to all the dreams I had
   Those wonderful, wonderful dreams?
The hopes and the expectations
   And the many elaborate schemes.

What happened to all the dreams I had?
   I was going to do it all,
I would live and laugh and be happy
   And really have a ball.

My plans were all mapped out for me
   I had so many expectations,
I faced life's challenges eagerly
   With hope and anticipation.

I welcomed life with open arms
   Holding tight to the pain and sorrow,
Knowing - or so I thought at the time
   That things would be better tomorrow.

I held all the hurt and pain inside,
   I hid all my dissatisfaction.
But little by little it grew and it grew
   And it grew as a chain reaction.

Now as the years have sidled by
   And my hopes have all turned to dust,
And my dreams have all disintegrated
   As little by little they must.

Little by little, it's fallen apart
  As little by little I died,
And little by little life's chipped away
  At my little bit of pride.

So this is the culmination of my youthful hopes and dreams,
The joyful expectations that must soon end - or so it seems.

Hazel Barber

DAWN UNSHARED

The pale and languid moon's adrowse with sleep
And wreathed around with mists of early dawn.
She's lulled by liquid notes of joyous birds
Proclaiming that another day is born.

The sun awakes and beams his fiery glee
At everything that he sees taking place.
His merriment's so coarse the moon retreats
And blushes stain the dawn sky's pallid face.

He roars out his approval of the world
And banishes each ling'ring trace of sleep.
Such is his mood that he at once forbids
His sister, Rain, her pearly tears to weep.

I stand here in the early morning cool
And watch him move, triumphant, through the sky
But his ascension brings no joy to me;
The vanquished moon detests him less than I.

I used to watch the sunrise once with you,
Remember, long ago, when you still cared?
What joy now can I gain from witnessing
The aching splendour of a dawn unshared?

Pauline Mackey

PUNCHLINE

We were damaged during the dawn of man.
How else were we s'posed to understand,
And grow and learn, as well?
How could we know Heaven
If we didn't know Hell?
Even love alone isn't pure.
Life is a disease and there is no cure.
We are bacteria experiencing hysteria
On the interior and exterior.
A bunion. A pimple.
On the simplicity of life's arse.
Don't talk to me about freedom.
We're the product of an author's farce.
A joke. A one-liner.
Not even a punchline.
Who's taking life seriously?
That life is not mine.
And still I joke and lie and laugh,
But, of course, the evil is but half
Of the whole picture
Hanging on God's wall.
We're the bacteria of hysteria.
That's all.
The Human Race: who's losing?
Is anyone winning?
Is anyone choosing,
Or is everybody sinning?
We were damaged during the dawn of time.
A cracker joke pulled from the Big Bang,
Never ending the punchline.

Antony Mapes

THE TASK

I gazed about the silent room
Then closed my eyes and made a sigh
I knew what lay ahead of me
A daunting task but I must try

With open eyes and baited breath
I turned my head and dared to look
And there it loomed in front of me
That dreaded task at which I shook

When faded eyes stared back at mine
I knew at once I must commence
Pale haggard skin, red glowing nose
The task was great, my body tense

And then as time began to pass
A peaceful ambience filled the room
I felt my body tension ease
And lightness push away the gloom

Those faded eyes were bright and clear
The haggard skin a rosy hue
The glowing nose a subtle pink
A transformation dream come true

The image in the mirror smiled
That happy radiant face was mine
Oh bless these days of beauty aids
The task fulfilled, success each time.

Sheila Wyatt

FRAGRANT GARDENS

Thoughts in a garden -
It must be hard when sense of smell is lost -
For the pleasure of fragrance counts the cost.
How *some* joy can be restored, if sight is lost -
Taking in the fragrance of a flower garden,
And the aromatic herbs perhaps grown therein.
Makers of toiletries the scents employ
In their wares - for us to 'freshen' and enjoy.
What would it be like without the flowers?
Some in regal state, some in overgrown 'bowers'!
'Queen' - the lily and the rose - perfect,
Which compels artists to beautifully depict -
Even those, for whom the use of hand, and arm, is lost -
Courage, so that the pleasure of their art will *not* be lost.
Sad thoughts - and - happy thoughts!

Mildred E Wood

WINTER WALK

Five o'clock on a winter's afternoon -
In the west the remains of the invisible sun
Slowly dim to pastel pinks, blues and greys.
At the end of the lane I turn to go home
And there ahead, the high-noon moon, centre stage,
now dominates the landscape,
Creeping up unseen while the sun was strutting his sunset glory.
Changing to silvered monochrome the world grows colder,
An ancient stillness and serenity enfolding the fields.
The few remaining pheasants slant to their roosts
And night has vanquished day.

Jennifer M Willmott

REMEMBRANCE - MIDDLE WALLOP 1984

A golden morning, yet the cold
incriminating frost has rimed the air,
icing the grass, hanging the hedgerows with
beaded medallions of the fading year.
In slow procession now they come,
behind the clergy, shell-shattered trophies
of the fight. The limbless, maimed, blind, the deaf,
the burned, precede the corporeally whole
who carry their wounds profoundly
in the soul. And in the moment's silence
the whole world holds its breath and listens to
the voices of the dead, an imminence
carried vocal upon the wind.
'Remember. Remember there can be no
forgiveness in forgetting. Remembrance
grants no liberty. Painfully we know
the mothers' hopes, those whose love
made death most terrible. The separate
agony of wives no longer rapt and
dreaming, the child alone and desolate,
deprived of love's inheritance,
and fathers drugged with life's placebo, pride.
These also bear war's wounds, lose dignity
and direction, it's in their names we chide.
Life's careless children do you heed
the lessons from catastrophes you seed?'
So poppy petals tumble from on high
to stain the air with crimson drops, like blood,
and pass into the future with a sigh.

M M Dolding

TRAFFIC AND THE SOLUTION

Above the horizon the sun will peep
Awakening all from the night's sleep
The jam-packed highways all in haste
Turning the tarmac into paste

What is gained by all the speed
Lots more accidents yes indeed
The air polluted with the fume
Cars nose to tail without room

How to stop it for a start
We could go back to horse and cart
A peaceful journey every day   .
And all this for a feed of hay

Ralph H Stephens

FREE BILLY

I know this may sound silly,
But when I met a man named Billy
I wished that I was he.
His hair was greasy, his eyes were squiffy,
And his aroma could only be described as whiffy,
But he was as happy as could be.
He gave me a smile, he gave me a wink,
And was not concerned about his stink.
He was so at peace with life.
So when I asked, 'Can you tell me please,
Dear Bill to what do you owe such ease?'
Bill replied, 'Eeeh I 'ave no wife.'

Marlene Parmenter

DAYDREAMING

On a bench in Mayflower Park with you,
I watch the waves, the seagulls, pigeons too.

The sun shines high in the sky,
Boats of all types and sizes pass by.

Children enjoy ice-cream, swim and play,
I thank God it's a heaven-sent day.

What would make my day complete, my dear,
Is a stroll with you along the pier.

The bygone days, through the turnstile I squeeze,
Catch some sun, feel the cool sea breeze.

In fancy wrought iron seat, I snooze,
And pretend I'm on a Queen Mary cruise.

I can enjoy a game of giant draughts,
Or 'trip' around the docks in pleasure crafts.

Relax in the restaurant for tea,
Visit the gift shop, knick-knacks to see.

Tomorrow the ferry to the Isle of Wight,
Back for the pavilion dance at night.

Yesteryear gone, the pier now in disrepair,
Like me most of Southampton folk really care.

Next door Mayflower Park is packed,
It should be so for the pier that's a fact!

Will the powers to be change their tune,
After all man has been to the moon!

Jenny Hayes

MOONLIGHTING

The total eclipse of a builder's bum
Is not a pretty sight
It's sometimes very pimpled
And almost always white

But we should not judge
These men in the building game
Just why their ill-fated trousers
Should rise and fall in vain

Their backsides are oblivious
To daylight and fresh air
A bottom doesn't know
When it has risen to be fair

It's a total mystery why
This apparition should appear
And why passers-by are so bemused
At the sight of a builder's rear

They never tell the builders
Of this gruesome, awesome sight
Could it be that they're too shy
Or maybe too polite

One thing is for certain
And this I have been told
It never gets frostbite
And rarely feels the cold

So next time you see a builder's bum
Please spare this thought in mind
His eye doesn't grieve what his eye can't see
So please tell him next time

Tony Stride

LIKE AN ANGEL

You really had such a lovely face
Filled with compassion and full of grace
You sparkled wherever you had to go
Like a lighted candle all aglow
Spreading joy and happiness around
Cheering people up when they were down
No matter who you came in contact with
Your motto was to give, give, give,
Give your love, give your smile, give your hand, pause a while
Give your heart, feel their pain, make them feel wanted again
You came here to spread deep love like an angel from above
You suffered, you knew pain but you managed to bounce back again
You made people realise there has to be love,
Human beings all need a reassuring hug
A kind word, a touch of a hand, you showed how to spread love around.
I hope from you people learn not to hurt each other or moan
But to follow the example set by you
Then your death which leaves us hurt and in pain
Would have been for a reason and not in vain,
You fulfilled what you came here to do
Now God has greater plans for you heading onwards towards the light
Watching over us, making sure we're doing things right
A shining star in the clear night sky, will remind us that you are nearby
I'll think of you and you'll be there, making me strong, making me care
You're only ever a thought away
Still smiling, still caring, still guiding us each day.

Vanessa Miller

TREES WITHOUT LEAVES

Autumn is cold but winter has a womb.

Nature's scrawl drained of
chromatics (love lingers in the wreckage).
Blown out. Showing ribs
it swamps the sky with nerves all
burst and sprayed.
A season of shrapnel (the
perfect time to breed analgesia).
Watch it grow

and fuse its arcs of anorexia to
inkspill branches sucked bloodclots drawn
out to needles and
daddy-long-legs' legs but darker.

It gets in the ears.
Breathes in tunnels
in time with traffic. It is
war footage shot by diabetics
(shaky sick at the edges).
It is feedback. It is memory. I remember

heart-monitor screams.
Lines left on a screen.

Tim Granville

IN MEMORIAM

Dead autumn leaves slide rustling,
As feet push through them scuffling
The myriad forms that nursed the trees
Gaily in the summer breeze.

New life bounds on ahead
No use waiting for the dead.
Behind, along the empty path
Misty images come into sight
Tails on high and brown eyes bright.
'Come on you two,' I call,
For we are still together as a pack
Just as surely as the dead leaves answer back.

Mary Allen

RUNAWAY

I feel that I could fly away
Collect my things and go
To a place where no one knows my name
Where I've neither friend nor foe.

I've felt like this a long time now,
There are many reasons why
And whenever I see a plane above
In the bright blue of the sky,
I yearn to be in a different place,
To start afresh somewhere,
In another town with a different name
Breathing different air.

Maybe one day I'll pack a bag
And me and my old guitar
Will hitch a lift or catch a train
To follow a different star.

Ann P Stevens

MIGRATION

Oh, take me with you where you fly,
On warm breezes through the sky.
Over mountain peaks with such a view,
Countryside glistening with morning dew,
To canyons deep where rivers flow,
To wondrous sights wherever you go.
Then bring me home through clouds of light,
And rest awhile before your next flight,
Your eyes so bright, your feathers shine,
Pleasure that's yours has also been mine,
So when you journey, far, alone,
Remember you're welcome always in my home,
Wherever that home is I will be,
Home is where the heart is, true for all to see.

L P Harrison

BLUE

Blue is the colour of a cloudless sky.
Blue is the glint in my mother's eye.
Blue is the sea, calm and still.
Blue is the lavender on the hill.
Blue is a sweet wrapper crinkled and square.
Blue is a balloon floating in the air.
Blue is my brother's fleece, warm and soft.
Blue is the ink in an inkpot.
Blue is the carpet where the cat lies.
Blue is the colour of dragonflies.
Blue is our car, shiny and new.
Blue is how I feel when I'm missing you.

Lucy Cross (11)

STRANGE STREETS, ON A DARK, EARLY MORNING

(On resettling in a new neighbourhood)

I have left my neighbours - those I knew;
Now: too many shadows darken strange doors.
Pools of faint, eerie light, from lone street lamps,
Show, dimly, pathways to the uncharted unknown,
Where ghostly cats arch their backs,
And fur bristles.

Unfamiliar pavement slabs and tarmac edges
Stub and trip my feet,
As I wander to learn of a new and foreign land;
Wondering what lies behind the window frames
With solitary lighted window panes,
And fully veiled sashes draped - alive with private mystique.

Lift those blinds. Pull back those veils.
Unfold me for those mysteries . . .
For I come amongst you as a friend -
A neighbour of good and sweet intent.
Brighten! your soulless light. Yes! - Unfold!
I only wish your hand to hold.

> The dawn edges up. - Shadows lessen.
> Curtain rails swish -
> There is a smile;
> A bland and puzzled stare.
> In hopeful reply, I nod and flap a hand -
> In an unfamiliar land of strange streets.

Come, horizon's dawn, full crack the sun.
Come, the jogger and the walker with dog,
The babbling children off to play or school.
I wish only to say: 'Good day'
And share a willing, friendly hand
To know the neighbours in my mysterious, foreign, new land.

William G Thomas

HIROSHIMA

It grew in many minds
A fission of ideas
To turn a million visions blind
And burn the skin with tears.
To kill through radiation
In many years to come,
To develop passionate hatred
In the unborn young.
They fought so many battles
That they knew would come with peace,
Sending marching men singing songs so loud
Above the stamping feet.
Away from home and away from friends
And over the distant hills,
Knowing they'd never return again
No matter how strong their will.
There's nothing any race can say -
It's one for one, no second place.
We all love life, yet steal it away
From others; mankind, the terminal case.

P D Edwards

BORDERS

The nomad halts at the edge of the desert,
And looks across -
His first sighting of an oil rig,

Huge - scratching the surface of the sky;
A giant quadrant charting the hemisphere -
Rich fat leaking from its fanning gills.

Needless of this thick, dark blood,
Pumped up from subterranean veins,
And gushing like laughter of Mohammed,

He applies a wisdom old as sand ripples:
Retreating to where the morning dissolved,
And the sun awakened him.

Derrick Porter

FAIRIES

All the fairies dance around,
In the trees and on the ground.
They make the fairy rings all day,
And then inside them they will play.

When you see a fairy light,
You'll find your smile will be so bright.
Fairies have continuous fun,
Each and every single one.

The fairies sing for you and me,
Sitting in the chestnut tree.
They love to trick and play around,
They love to hide and to be found.

Come the night and time to sleep,
Not one fairy dares to peep.
Await the early morning call,
When fairies wake, one and all.

Now please do not be a fool,
Follow this quite simple rule.
Never say a fairy's name,
For they will never be the same.

Lauren Zabiela (13)

FULL CIRCLE

No Escort on the driveway, nobody coming in,
No ciggies on the doorstep, no dog-ends in the bin . . .
The house is strangely quiet, and rooms stay neat and clean,
A flattened patch of carpet shows where the hi-fi's been.
Computer, books, and boxes are safely moved away,
Her cuddly toys and teddies no longer on display,
The washing pile's diminished, and ironing's quick to do,
No long hairs in the bathroom, no waiting for the loo!
The supermarket trolly's now full of calories,
Not low-fat yoghurts, lagers, and countless 'sugar-frees' . . .
The tele is neglected, the phone is rarely touched,
I seldom boil the kettle, and don't drink tea as much.   .
The biscuit tin's not empty, the fridge is tightly stacked,
The freezer's full to bursting, the larder's closely packed.
I'm using smaller saucepans when cooking meals at night,
But one less place at table still doesn't feel quite right . . .
I miss our lively gossips about the day's events,
And 'girlie' times out shopping at Master Card's expense!
For years I've loved and cherished to make this house a home,
And now my daughter's left it - and bought one of her own!

Rosemary Ann Shaw

SPRING CLEAN

Why must I dream my life away?
Why can't I live just for today?
It seems my life needs a good spring clean
What I'd give for a change of scene
I must find strength to change my life
To rid myself of stress and strife
For then I know that I would find
True happiness and peace of mind.

Geoffrey Lindley

CORN DOLLY

Above the pewter and willow pattern plate
Lining the walls
She stands alone on a little shelf:
Serene and beautiful
Hands raised in ancient benediction
Over the shopping-laden wives
Sipping coffee on market days.
This maid of the golden skirt
Pleated and woven by deft hands
Is not just the stalks of last year's harvest
Given life by skilled fingers:
She is the symbol of continuity
Linking past beliefs and rites
To present day.
Children gaze, fascinated,
Eyes wide in wonder at the story
Which they, in turn, will relate
To the unborn generations.

Jennifer A Ackerman

TO CHLOE

Christmas Day saw your arrival,
Welcome! To the game, survival.
Pretty face, with eyes of blue,
We all wish the *best* for you.
As you grow, in body and mind,
Goodness in everyone, may you find,
May you learn what's right and wrong,
Darling girl, you living song,
Grow in grace, enjoy your life
And avoid unpleasant strife.

Mamorald

THE WEDDING DRESS

She unwrapped the tissue, and shook out every fold.
It was no longer shining white, but softly burnished gold.
The smell of lavender wafted on the air,
And a few dried traces of it, still were lingering there!

She held the dress against her, and danced around the floor,
Her thoughts were all of yesteryear, with memories galore!
The waistband looked so tiny, had she really been that small?
And she was sure the buttons, would never reach at all!

The years had passed so quickly, since she became a wife,
The time before her marriage seemed someone else's life!
The young man, who had claimed her, as his 'Blushing Bride'
Forty years now, later, was still walking at her side!

She was humming softly, as she glided, to and fro.
'Twas the music that was played, on that day, so long ago.
She remembered all the trouble she'd had, 'putting up hair',
And could see her father's face, as she'd come down the stair.

As she'd left her parents' cottage, that stood on the village green,
Her father had whispered softly, that she, 'Looked just like a queen!'
The organ started playing, as they'd entered the church gate,
As she'd come to join her sweetheart, on their most important date!

They had raised a lively family, in all the years between -
The eldest being thirty-eight, the youngest, seventeen.
There'd been several little babies, in the last five years or so,
And she was watching fondly, a new generation grow!

She gave a final twirl, in her dance across the floor,
And turned, to see him watching, from beside the open door!
He gave his gentle smile, and stretched out his loving arms,
And she melted, once again, beneath the magic of his charms!

Jeannette R D Jones

I MISS

I miss those moments of intimate elation
I have nothing to show except constant frustration
I miss the comfort of your cradling arms
Sedating my fears
Reducing my tears
I miss the gentle embrace
The summer in your face
Your kiss so full of grace
I miss the hand that held me tight
My desolate land have no stars at night
I miss the speech of inspired dreams
A reality once relished, swept downstream
I miss the soothing breath which sealed my soul
Your sensual seduction which healed life's hole
I miss the delicate stroke from your fingertips
The words you spoke from those whispering lips
I miss the lingering stare
The moments we shared
A vacant space that's no longer there
I miss you

Marcus W Bailey

RETURNING

The car high-stepping the winding rain-soaked road,
wipers combating blurred vision,
wheels tattooing a wet rhythm.
Each motorist isolated in the spume,
a tedious, monotonous follow-my-leader
under dark sodden skies.
The cassette fills our womb-like world with glorious sound.
Energy, momentum,
we're homeward bound.

Ellsie Russell

THE BATTLE OF TOTTON

Day or night, it wouldn't have mattered how much
Or how little light, but the darkness seemed to
Lend an extra little something to the tense
And bitter fight.

The wind was keen and mighty, spirited and determined.
The flags seethed.

Drawing air, the wind grew; gathering speed, it swept
In from the sea. Buffeting rooftops, bullying
Chimneys and filling trees. It ballooned and bounded,
Seized the limp cloth, and tore in.

Ready or not, it wouldn't have mattered who the flags
Were for; where they were, why they were there,
Or the badges that they wore.

But there they were, and up for it
Mad, now, strong-willed and spitting.
The wind mocked and toyed.

The wind wound and coiled, and sprang;
The flags unfurled; straining at their posts.
The wind attacked again. The flags resisted.
They wrestled like demons; demented souls released.

Freaking like fits; ripping into one another.
Embroiled like some crazy allergic reaction.
First one, then the other. Tearing like terriers;
Snapping like tempers, but worse.

And then, in one final, ironic twist, calm.
The wind dropped and the flags fell.
The dizzy spell passed and settled
Weather moved in, over West Cliff.

Stephen Palfrey

BLUES

I'm not sixteen, I'm umpty-four,
Just not a spring chick any more,
I'm not the age that men adore -
I've got the middle-age menopause blues!
The lines are showing on my face,
My figure's just a darn disgrace
Feel like the oil-rag round this place
I've got the middle-age menopause blues.
I'm feeling like a dying swan
My go-gpo-go's all gone-gone-gone
And just sweet memories linger on
I've got the middle-aged menopause blues.
I've quite mislaid my youthful zest -
I dare not put it to the test.
Where *did* I put my woolly vest?
I've got the middle-age menopause blues.
They say that life begins again
When you reach the age of four times ten.
But they don't say how long it lasts:
I hope these doldrums soon will pass
(I've got the middle-age menopause blues)
The men all look much younger now;
I feel like 'whoa' instead of 'wow'!
Back yourself up, you silly cow,
You've got the middle-age menopause blues!

Val Carter

As Time Goes By

As one gets advanced in years
One tries to live, shedding a few less tears,
After various bouts of sadness
There usually appears to be more gladness.
It did for me, although I had almost given up hope
As all I seemed to do was grope.
I met a gentleman who became my friend
And at last my loneliness came to an end.
He too, like me, had lost his mate
So to go out for a day we would make a date
He like me is visually impaired,
So we chat and get our problems aired.
There are times we need to read a time-table
But find neither of us are able.
We laugh and find it all a huge joke,
And I am so pleased that I met that 'bloke'.

Frances M Jenkins

Lovers

One soul dwelling in two bodies,
Separate, yet together,
With moments of love;
One heart as one whole,
Separate as yearning parts,
Just incomplete;
Two bodies entwined as one being,
Always loving and true;
Two minds thinking alike,
Thinking and feeling the same,
Yet individual;
Two lives existing incomplete,
Without the other's love.

Sharon Cooper

THE HAWKHURST GANG

Keeping sheep
By moonlight
A past-time
Cold and chill

They hung
My poor tired body
In chains
Upon the hill

To feed my wife
And children
I took
But a share

(With a degree
Of stealth)
The surplus
Of the rich man's ware

They showed
To me
No mercy
But hung me here

On high
In chains
Upon the hillside

No one to heed my cry . . .

T F White

ABOUT SAM

Sweet boy.
Oh, my dear!
Ambiguous boy.
Outrageous!

Speed!
Thrill!
Too fast - too fast!

The carnage of your death
So incongruous
With your gentle life.

Friends weep.
Bewildered.
Simple expedition for a new hat
At that last meeting
Remembered and revered.
Searching for a photograph.
Holding on - holding on
To you.

You have deprived us
Of your career.
Oh, but what a performance.
What a splendid finale.
Like St Joan.

Sweet boy.
Oh, my dear!
Ambiguous boy.
Outrageous!

M J Ray

THE MAGIC OF THE RUINS

The rusting hinges creak for very age,
The great oak door - a shadow of its former self,
Swings to and fro on gentle breeze,
Opening to view the crumbling ruins,
Dank, deserted, vandalised by centuries of time.

Here once a great cathedral stood,
Here men and women knelt in prayer,
There stood the altar all resplendent
With its cloth of purest white
Embroidered with a thread of glittering gold.

Here stood the priest, the chalice lifted high,
A poignant symbol of the Saviour's act of love;
While gently wafted on the scented air
Sweet music weaved its magic spell.

Today there is no priest, no celebrants,
The altar stands there bare - no cloth of broidered gold,
Its ancient stone bathed in mystic light,
The rays of summer sun dancing through stained and shattered panes.

My mind hears music, soft and low,
Drifting on the summer breeze,
As if the organ can no longer silence keep;
While choral harmony, so long unheard,
Rises sweetly towards the azure vault.

In reverence I kneel among the ruins there,
And in my heart a silent prayer,
Thanking the Father for the Saviour's selfless love,
And for the hope this brings of life from heaven above.

Ray Millier

TRUE LOVE ˙

I am fast approaching eighty-one -
Not that I feel that old.
Now that I'm getting on a bit
Memories begin to unfold.
I remember the days of the cycling club -
In particular 'the light of my life'.
He had dark brown eyes and a gorgeous smile
And I vowed I'd become his wife.
But that was sixty-two years ago
And we parted because of the war.
He went to serve in Burma
Whilst I served here on our shore.
The years passed by - forty in all
And then, one day, I received a call.
He was back, alive, I would see him again,
Gone was the sadness, the worry and pain.
My prayers have been answered,
My dreams have come to life.
We are once again together
As a loving husband and wife.

Irene Kelsey

MEMORIES

Wistful eyes of a three year old
Looked down on the scene below
Little urchins were sitting on the curb -
Outside the pub: across the road.

Long, unwashed hair, framed grubby faces,
Worn-out shoes - with broken laces.
Dirty dresses - tattered and torn,
Boys - wearing trousers, big brothers had worn.

How I longed to be there with them all,
But my Mum was disgusted and dragged me away
So I shouldn't see the shocking display
As the parents came out, at the end of the day
Some of them drunk -
'Cause they'd spent all their pay.

Laura Harris

SHINGLE LINES

The gnawing ragged shingle lines,
Shall pull your strings come summertime
And drag you down without regret.
Your feet shall follow one by one
And tempt your soul to warm and wet,
And as those winged beasts shall cry.
The spray will kiss your crimson eyes.
Once my heart shall miss a beat,
Then all the world to know my dreams,
Will dance behind my marching feet.
And now,
All is not left to wail
Against that pinnacle of shale,
But simply to digest your mind
And pull your strings come summertime,
Or satisfy and bring to light
A dancing wind,
A laughing sky,
Or maybe just an endless night.

John Matthews

A Prodigal Daughter Of Plymouth

Return to rue the day that I ever left its leafy ways
And quays, sorrow driven to me by city bright with streets of gold
And upper hype, lessons hard I had to learn, to my fairy city
                                        - Plymouth return.
Wasted years on pavements drear, silence where there should
                                        have been cheer,
Hardship, poverty, disease: mine enemies to me did displease.
I thought of Thais, thought of Ishtar, thought of Isis as a distant star
And oh! How I longed to return to the city of Drake and the
                                        crescent burn.
Nazi planes did bomb and blitz the brethren of this city of bliss,
Where valiant men and women gave their very lives our souls to save.
St Andrew's now, a place of rest where worshippers may worship best
Who love the Lord with *all* their might and fear His wrath,
                                        as so they might.
Come memories of Dad and Mum, gentle pleasures beneath the sun,
Noble they in spirit bore, three little ones as though before
No family bonded in such sad dismay, for now we are parted
                                        and gone our ways.
I learned my lessons well, I say to my Father, 'Here I dwell,'
Beside the sea and utter peace with gulls around me, gone is grief,
But in my heart I always roam upon the moors which once was home
Where swallows flew and bark did thicken on the trees
                                        the buds did quicken
Hedge and hedgerow growing by and silver larch to reach the sky.

I did not earn that hard cash which the wanton city calls its stash.
Where markets crumble into dust, I placed my jewels in heaven,
                                        if I must:

Believe me, there were tears that rang but in my heart I heard
her refrain;
'Like me, she longs to come again to Camelot.' Have I not seen
her in the prow
Singing her song and the winds that sow, for the leaves that fall about
Like Ophelia's flowers give shout, to Love that is Enduring True;
To my God and to my city too, I say: 'Please forgive me, I love you.'

Joy Sheridan

UNTITLED

We've had a good life, lass.
Not perfect by any means,
but then,
we didn't expect it to be.

We had a strong marriage, girl,
in trial and in error,
lovers and friends, friends and lovers.

We've done well, love.
We might never have been rich;
nevertheless,
we had a gem beyond price.

Aye, we made a good team.
We shared the load between us,
and we've got some good kids.

It's time to move on, now.
Come on, lass, hold my hand.
We'll watch the sunrise together one last time,
and then
I'll take you home.

Ruth Liddemore

RURAL DORSET

Along wooded lanes and leafy tracks
I often spend my day
to hear the birdsong and see the deer
with rabbits, badgers and foxes too
all busy at their play
for this be Dorset with nature at its best.
You walk a mile then glimpse
the sea all shimmering in the sun
with luck perhaps you may espy some
dolphins having fun.
With Golden Cap and Portland Bill
and places in between
all there for eyes to see and
Abbotsbury with all its swans,
the Fleet and Chesil beach
add to this hazy scene.
What chance a linnet or a warbler
perched on a leafy branch
with wary eye for birds of prey
for they're never far away.
Soft warm winds and ripening corn
add to this lovely day
'Tis Dorset on a summer's morn
enjoyed by all that stay.

Leonard Timbury

THE POPPY

The poppy and what it means to me
It's the blood of many soldiers
Who fought to keep us free
Its petals red as blood of the men
Who died in war
Sons, husbands, lovers, alas
They are no more
It's a simple wayside flower
Which grows in fields of green
But they were stained with blood
In the year nineteen seventeen
On the field of Flanders a bloody
Battle was fought in vain
Too few against so many
They never fought again
Now every year on Remembrance Day
In London's Albert Hall
The service men and women stand still
As stone, as the petals softly fall
They fall in their hundreds upon hundreds
One for every man who died
In the First World War and the Second World
War and many more beside
The petals fall from that blood red flower
And many a tear flows down
For the blood of men and the poppies red
Are mingled in a field of brown
Yes! This simple wayside flower that grows
In fields all across our lands
Like carpets of blood from the men who
Died in those distant far off lands

Sheila Chimes

VISITING DAY

I watch their faces young and old
Some are sad, some are bold,
Through the door and across the hall
Select a table and that is all,
Then they sit and wait.

Then a movement from across the room
All heads turn as one, and soon
A sound of keys, as a lock is turned
And a man appears, a visit earned.

Their faces light with a joyous smile
The long cold journey has been worthwhile,
The hall now fills with murmuring sounds
While the silent watchers stand around.

Children play not caring much,
While parents talk and smile and touch,
For when they part as they must do
There's only memories to see them through.

As I walk out towards the sea,
I am so glad that I am free.

Joan Perry

THE VETERINARY NURSE

Thank you for your caring hands,
Caring hands and loving heart,
Tenderly you cared for me
When I was frail and weak,
But you were strong and kind,
Long hours you nursed me patiently,
You didn't mind.

Thank you for your gentle touch,
Gentle touch and smiling eyes,
Skilfully you nurtured me
Through brokenness and strife.
Healing gifts of love you gave.
Never wearying.
Your aim - protect and save.

Christine Ahern

AT THE SHEPHERDS' FIELD

Not far from Bethlehem you find the field,
The place where shepherds watched their flocks, it's said,
Near the old road, which makes its busy way,
Jerusalem to this town, 'the House of Bread'.

It won its name because when travellers passed
The barren hills above the lifeless sea
They reached with thankfulness this ancient town
Where they well knew water and food would be.

We gathered in the field on Christmas Eve -
A level space, some way below the road -
How lit, I now forget; stars overhead;
The lights of Bethlehem on the hilltop showed.

We pictured shepherds round their flickering fire,
Chatting of all the folk the Census brought.
'When will Messiah come?' they may have said,
Recalling prophesies their Rabbis taught.

What visions were they shown, these simple men,
Which set them urgently to climb the hill?
'They came with haste' breathless and full of hope,
And where they knelt, 'all people' worship still.

Kathleen M Hatton

Sea Change

From early morning
Sparkling turquoise waves
Edged with foamy lace
Whisper sea-songs
Under the gold
Of a summer sun

Day recedes
Dusk advances
Water agate-green
Now slaps and surges
Over ancient pebbles
On a lonely beach

In the looming cliffs
Strange fossils
Lie undisturbed
Through millennia
Keeping their secrets
Of a lost time

Feeding fish
Come to the surface
Their scaly beauty
Gleaming jewel-bright
In the diamond light
Of a midnight moon

Barbara Brookes

BARMITZVAH

Master of Ceremonies
Announces each Guest
Millions of Pennies
My Bar Mitzvah's Best
Handshakes and Presents Galore
Envelopes stashed in pocket
Yesterday I couldn't ask more
I took off like a Rocket
Noah was the portion I read
Synagogue full - Family around
Now all Guests are well fed
Here on Greshams home ground
Laughter, Smiles and Pleasantries
Happiness fills each room
Champagne, Whisky and Canapés
My Father's voice does boom
Chandeliers all shining bright
Evening Dress - Plenty of Jewels
This is my Celebratory Night
Wits, Rabbinics, Jesters and Fools
All enjoy the company assembled
Yet how I remember the night before
I stood in my room and trembled
Lest a mistake I make in reading the Law
But Sunny aspect did embrace
The Shabbas of my maturity
Apparently shone on my radiant face
One of innocence and purity
Now the Band strikes up
So Dance we will until Midnight
Fill each and every friendly cup
With Torah's Shining Light.

Michael Stewart Rivlin

THE JOY OF LIFE

Life is such a complicated thing
Even though much joy it brings
There is so very much to learn,
I don't know which way first to turn
One day I'm up - one day I'm down
Sometimes I smile - sometimes I frown.
I wish someone would explain to me
The way things really ought to be.
It's hard I guess, but I must learn
By myself which way to turn.
As life goes by and problems come,
I will learn to solve them one by one.
Life brings such joy, love and hope
And as I slowly learn to cope
With every little stress and strain
Life to me seems just great again.

Liz Charge

MOONLIGHT ON LULWORTH COVE

I wish you had looked through your window last night
Nature was displaying a wonderful sight
The cove shimmered like a floodlit stage
Looking more beautiful than any brochure page.

A fox moved stealthily over nearby grass
Waiting anxiously for a cloud to pass
Across the moon, and obscure his way
So that he might unseen, pursue his prey.

The white chalky path beckoned me to tread
My way to the top, towards Bats Head.
The moonlit sight filled me with total awe
As I scanned the coast from Mupe to Durdle Door.

A stunning silence pervaded the air
I really wished you had been there to share
This magical, wonderful, God-given night
But you slept on, with your curtains shut tight.

Devina Symes

APPRENTICESHIP

Like the hammer at the forge,
the bellows to the fire;
like the plough to the field;
like sight to desire;
like cogs to machines,
the spoke-shave to the wheel;
like the last to the cobbler,
hard-bargaining to the deal.
But, also perhaps,
like frost to the cobweb,
the kitten to string,
sunset to the night sky,
the owl to hunting;
like the lapwing to the misty furrow,
the swift to migration,
its cup to the acorn;
like the tiny seed to the good earth,
the spade to the garden;
like the doorway to departure,
the licking flame to the stubble,
today to tomorrow
and the generous heart to sorrow.

M J Robbins

A POEM OF LOVE

You are safe within my heart
Where the flame of love is burning

You can feel the warmth in my embrace
When I hold you tight.

You can feel passion in my kiss
The taste of love is on my lips.

You look deep into my eyes
Where compassion lies.

My whole being is full of love
For you that overflows and fills the air.

I love you.

C J Walls

AFTER MORNING SERVICE

After morning service we would walk for miles;
Outside the village, over stiles
And up a softly sloping hill
Where violets hid beneath the hedge, till,
From the top, we could look out across the trees
To where the ocean skittered in the breeze.
And if there ever had been any doubt -
What, we had wondered, was it all about -
It soon dissolved itself, faced with the drama
Of that supernal panorama.

Dorothy Davis-Sellick

THE RESTLESS HEART

The doors are open wide this evening
To the motionless air;
After the windy day the clouds are disbanded
And fled away over the receding land,
The stars shine out like glinting plates
Reflected in the fire-lit room,
The sheep-trod turf makes muted feet.
Each blade of grass and each ear of wheat
Stand perpendicular to the sky
And leaves, like steel shavings, stick
To the sparse, individual sleeping trees;
Darkness closes the distance of the hills;
The birds are still.
Our voices murmur and the receptive mind
Listens
As each thought projects
Ideas and images of a childhood's past.

Tonight is as other immemorial summer nights;
The path, too, to the marsh must have borne
Numerous other persons on their way
And our hearts, like those other men's, who can say,
Beat on, restless
Stimulating the mind that springs
To richer, stranger and more marvellous things
That we in dreams have felt
But in our childhood knew.

Paul Gardner

PAMIR AT SEA

Out of a trough now the foretruck emerges,
royal and double t'gallants appear,
followed by topsails (and they too are doubled)
then the huge forecourse and bowsprit break clear.

Sped by a trade wind now fair on her taffrail,
racing she runs for the next deep ravine;
dipping her forefoot, submerging her scuppers,
blue giving way to sub-aqueous green.

Free once again, her canvas soon filling,
chanting the shanty all sailing ships sing,
all aboard know that by sufferance only
may progress be made where Neptune is king.

Lovely and lethal, she heads for a landfall,
ready to strike at the first careless act -
send a man plummeting down from a yardarm,
douse him and drown him ere she is turned back.

That is a risk that all sailors must take who
wish above all from the land to be free;
courting each time when they leave home and safety,
Satan's own doxy - the volatile sea.

T C Hudson

THEN AND NOW

Stone slowly yielding
To dust-covered quarrymen.
Life blood of Portland.

Stone crushed unheeded
By oil-smeared machinery.
Life blood declining.

Gillian Ford

IN THE DEEP OF WINTER

In the deep of winter, where wind and rain do dwell
  Oft there is seen a glimmer, when log fires burn
And grey smoke yearns its way toward low cloud so still

See the trees gaunt and grey, watch them bend and sway
  Taunted by cold wet winds, searching through woodland and lane
Turning dead leaves and causing endless tears on warm window panes

And when at last snow her white carpet fast falls
  No ye winter is finale come, hear again children's long awaited
                                        happy cries
Watch them slide and sleigh, follow footsteps down icy pathways.

Feel the quiet of winter's white, see the colour of birds set in the
                                        midst of snow's piercing light
  Venture through the streets of town, watch the people wrapped
                                        in heavy clothes
Dashing to and fro, lest cold should fingers bite
  Snow laid roofs so warm they seem, like winter's scarf a
                                        cotton wool dream

Too soon it melts and runs away, distorted snowmen, slush and ice
  Workmen with noisy shovels clear away, 'What's next?' They say
Yes, what weather now will pass this way
  Come the end of February, winds heave and rain showers try
Monday's washing has no time to dry

Curtains drawn early inside houses, where dim lights shine
  Cat and dogs too, lie by wood fires embered glow
But nature, she stirs, flowers begin to shoot, bulbs first blooms
                                        already they do show
  Could it be that winter has turned her ageing head so bare
Yes, deep winter see it there, has finale given way, with spring,
                                        she now shares.

Roy Wootton

GO AWAY

Doorbell ringing . . .
If I don't know who it is, shall I answer it,
Do I want to find out, or shall I just sit
Until they go away?

Telephone ringing . . .
Have I been waiting to hear for so long,
Do I want to know who, or let it go on
Until the utter silence?

Alarm clock . . .
Will the world stop if I throw it at the wall,
If I disappear in the blankets will it matter at all?
I'll simply lose my job.

Bells ringing . . .
Sometimes in my head, and sometimes real
Beautiful church bells make me feel
Uneasy.

Always summons . . .
Peal and chime
Watch the time
Ding-dong
Hurry along,
Clock - church - doorbell - and phone
How would it be
if you left me
alone?

Joanna Carr

REQUIEM ON PETT BEACH

Aside the desolate breaks of rock and sand,
  ravaged by winds and countless tides,
I stand curiously exposed, like some small crab
  unkindly left in daylight.

Sand, thrust upwards by a savage wind,
  grazes my skin.
Spray stings the eyes.
Stranded seaweed gropes its gnarled fingers,
  seeking the solace of deep pools.
The horizon split by heaving waves
  lies like broken glass.
Spume, spitting grained marble at the rocks
  creams the waters.
Along the shore-line marsh grasses spear the air
  shrieking spiked noise
  into the volume of grey space.
A lone salt-thrown Tamarisk sideways leans,
  its feathery foliage flicking into the crash of air
  sound echoes
  screaming a chorus of souls' despair.

Whipped by an alien force in this
  unsheltered place.
Surrounded by a primitive nakedness,
  nature, in her element, storms my day apart.
I find myself buffeted by loneliness and fear.
I came only to walk and be alone.
Yet, in this vast beloved waste
  I comprehend.
This too, could be the beginning of the end of me.

Janine Vallor

CRETAN STORM

Oiled bodies by the pool,
Rows of bent knees roasting,
Couples squealing in blue water,
Under a lazy summer sky;
Cicadas rasp their washboards,
Sprinklers hiss on nearby lawns.
But clouds are looming . . .
Sky muddies,
Distant mountains fade,
Flashes split the air,
Dispersing the relaxing crowds.
Thunder gods drop trays above,
Windows rattle,
Hammering rain floods pathways,
Sunbathers cower in their rooms.
At last heavenly anger ceases.
Laughing hooded figures splash through lakes,
The mountains return,
And a corner of the sky gleams.

Julia Perren

PASTURES OF THE SKY

Again I've come to the dream-dark
trail on the tall bow-bend's mantle
to find the twilit sky awake
with thistledown of cumulus
swift off the bay's broken roundel.

Like caterpillar-silk, the cloud
owns beads of starlight while, behind,
the town stains it with its own crude
daylight and a dusting of rouge:
I face the sea, town out of mind.

Ungrazed at present these fields bloom
still with their lapis lazuli
stolen from day, binding the loam
and clay of distant cloud, like spring
and the bells it rings to the eye.

Yet this is winter: the solstice
approaches like a fawn oak leaf
down an old river, as though place
were merely a thought, jettisoned.
No: it's as rooted as a cliff.

Chris White

CHRISTCHURCH

From the busy streets of London I did come down,
To nurse in this little sleepy town.
I was asked many times if I ever regretted it,
The answer was always 'No', not one little bit.

Nursing children or old folk you are supposed to get more rest,
'Oh well you think, the powers that be should know best'.
They must have forgotten how unpredictable these folk can be,
But at least there was always laughter for others to see.

I loved medical nursing from time to time,
Then few were hurt should I burst into rhyme.
You see I took up nursing as I wished to care,
And bring these tranquil surroundings for all who wished to hear.

Christchurch hospital had an atmosphere that couldn't have been better,
Though all procedures were carried through to the letter.
The patients were happy and to them it was home,
But naturally this didn't always go down well with some.

Betty Green

THE COMMON 1940

A lark still sings
On beating wings
High in the dust-swept air.
But a hare leaps up
For its young to suck
Too weak to reach its lair.
Once a heron flew lowering
Over heather flowering
And grasses were springing
On the marsh.
Once a curlew sang trilling
Its long piping thrilling
As its calling was lost
In the mist.
But a heron can seem like an omen.

Now tank-tracks have churned
And trees have been burned
Scarring the beautiful land.
I suppose one might say
We are back to the clay.
Will we ever be human again?

Elizabeth Rainsford

FOLKESTONE

Let us go again to Folkestone
And sit upon the Leas.
We'll find ourselves a grassy nook,
That's sheltered by the trees.

We'll gaze again across the sea,
We'll watch the ships sail by,
See through the maze of sweet wild flowers
The pale blue Butterfly.

The sea will glisten 'neath the sun,
The waves will break below,
And through the winding hidden paths
Light-hearted we may go.

Valerie Small

THE GREAT ESCAPE

*(Based on a true episode which happened in North Wiltshire
and made the headlines)*

One day in deepest Wiltshire
Some pigs to slaughter went.
The two Tamworths among them
Were out on mischief bent.

They laid their plans so carefully
For this amazing stunt;
When coast was clear, the ringleader
Would signal with a grunt.

So when the crucial moment came
And door was left ajar,
Their trotters barely touched the ground
As they raced off afar.

They swam the river Avon
Their courage plain to see;
They scuttled through the countryside
Delighted to be free.

They landed in a woody copse
Puffed out and rather shaken;
But soon were grunting happily
At least they'd saved their bacon!

Joyce Reeves Holloway

IDENTITY OF A SOLDIER

I am a soldier, the men of Rome defeated us
and their legions filled us all with fear
but we became one nation welded by the years.
I am a soldier, we Britons had no army
so we could not defeat these Saxon men,
I married a Saxon woman, six hundred years
sped by, I am now an Englishman.
I am a soldier, I fought the Vikings up at
Stanford bridge, and we rejoiced - then a
forced march south exhausted, to fight once more
the Normans up on Senlac Hill, but they killed
our king, then we fought them in the thickets
and in woods, then rebellion in the north again
we paid heavily in blood.
I am a soldier, I fought at Agingcourt and Crecy
leaving many thousands dead.
Then we fought amongst ourselves - in the battles
of the white rose and the red,
then again between parliament and king.
I am a solider, I have fought in battles in the
east, in Africa and in all the world, far from
this place called home, to forge a mighty empire
greater far than Rome's.
I am a soldier, I have fought in two world wars,
has the world grown sick of men like me?
Though the wars are smaller now, the world still bleeds.
Sometimes I wonder - when can I say, I am no more
a soldier.

Howard Gibbs

LOOKING OUT

I watched the snowflakes falling,
And settle on the ground,
Making a white blanket,
Everywhere around.

The snow was getting thicker,
And the air is colder too,
My thanks to them that brave it,
Because of the work they do.

I also watch the other folk,
Who just go out for fun,
It reminds me of bygone days,
When I was also young.

The snow is now compacting,
And danger does abound,
The rear end of that lorry,
Is slowly sliding round.

That lovely white blanket,
Has now turned into ice,
Play is all now finished,
And the scenery not so nice.

Let's pray a rise in temperature,
Will clear away this mess,
And things get back to normal,
The danger is far less.

Will A Tilyard

INNOCENT LOVE

You have the voice of an angel,
You hold the beauty of a dream.
Everything about you is perfect,
Inevitably, you are supreme.
You're everything I ever dreamed of,
Plus a thousand things more.
You seem to touch inside my soul,
I have never known of this before.
You are young, you're talented, you're able,
You are worlds apart from me.
In my heart remains a hope,
That one day, together we'll be.
I sit alone, imagining,
Whilst you are adored by screaming fans.
I'll never be close by your side,
I'll just admire in a distant land.
Your eyes sparkle in the spotlight,
Your lips pout when you sing,
You're so graceful in all you do,
You could be a dove without wings.
The pain I receive from needing you,
The loneliness inside my heart.
This love that's grown is ready to perform,
You're the one I want to play the part.

Kate Boud

TO THE WORLD'S CHILDREN

We have failed you . . .
Your inheritance,
A world of wars rooted in religions
Mouthing creeds of brotherly love,
Feuds fought in the name of justice
Reeking of hatred and intolerance.

More threatening than global warming
The sadists' insidious poison
More menacing that meteoric strikes
The fanatics' determination.

We are so weary of strife, so tired of turmoil
Faced with our failure
In what can we ask you to believe?

And yet -
The soaring wonder of snow-capped mountains
Still arrests,
Trees and flowers of heart-stopping beauty,
Give us hope,
Remind us of life's continuum.

Learn from our mistakes.
With care and compassion
Use the amazing new technology
Savour life's true riches . . .
Companionship, love of family and friends.
Accept kindnesses proffered,
Give freely of goodwill to all,
Regardless of colour or creed.

This amazing multi-faceted universe is yours.
In it may you find joy and peace.

Vera Morrill

JOURNEY'S END

We are all gone now, you and I
Through the hidden days and pathways
That held us safe and sleeping
Challenged the light that we may see
Desperate glory, like mist, unfolding
Together, without thoughts provoking
Nothing, but this we held
This short, bewitching span of life
Dance with death and wait the motionless tide
Our souls would soar and kiss the stars
Falling, between the lines of black and white
Are we now so changed, we cannot see
Time that slips against the day
Pale, translucent lights, bathed in unkissed pools
We bask in sunlight
Forsake the dead to cold sleeping
Cast away the flame edged tears
Winds that broken arrows call to rest
Feel us no more, our empty breath
We are a silent, unremembered place
For we are all gone now, you and I.

C A Gregory

FRIENDSHIP

This moment has
just gone, passed by
drifted into another place.
For time itself crosses
through lives and memories.
We are all searching for love,
a love that cannot be soured.

Never let the opportunity
to make friends for friendship's sake
go by,
or you'll have regrets.
For something lost
May never be found.
Inside you would have been richer.

Michael Wilson

OWL'S ROOST

If only we could still be there -
That lovely cottage - standing where
The fields of flowers just like a carpet in the spring,
The memories all come flooding in,
The massive walnut tree (but still so old).
Providing the squirrel of rusty gold -
With a winter store of sheer delight -
Collected in the dead of night.
Then in the morning, eager hands collect them all
From the hole that's made by the privy wall.
There are oaks to climb, to shout and sing -
Helping out the rooks fierce din.
The baker man with a horse and cart
Whistling his way with a merry march.
Stopping to let the horse drink from the stream
Listening to the songbirds scream of sheer delight - but as yet unseen,
They all congregate at the top of the trees
And look up to heaven - feeling the breeze.
They are thinking it's wonderful to be alive
Giving pleasure to all - as they make a dive.
To the field where 'Owl's Roost' once majestically stood,
Making me stop and think of memories so good.

Iris J Brown

A HOMAGE TO MUSIC

On the hi-fi or car stereo,
Music follows me, wherever I go.
Hear the musicians, play beats to the bar,
Sometimes we sing, and sometimes we la.
Quavers and crotchets, leap out of the page,
As glorious melodies, are heard from a stage.
Is it an orchestra, sounding so grand,
Or some keyboard whiz-kid, his own One Man Band.
For rock fans the beat, and for soul fans the base,
Whatever the music, these sounds have their place.
Just once in a while, an expert of rhyme,
Will write a song lyric, to last for all time.
Panpipes sound haunting, hear the soulful sax,
Why not try classical, it helps to relax.
Woofers and Tweeters, have a new lease of life,
Turn them up loud, give the neighbours some strife.
It could be the radio, or maybe CD,
But one thing's for sure, it's fulfilment to me.

A D Beaumont

PENCARROW HEAD - CORNWALL

A little bit of heaven
Five miles or so, no more -
Where heath and gorse and bracken
Reach down to hug the shore.
A rock-strewn curving coastline,
With paths of shale and scree
Fringed by a lace of foaming water
As far as the eye can see.
An undulating pathway
Exciting to the tread
As it twists and turns and teases
For new vistas just ahead.

Pencarrow Head has charmed me
For some twenty years or more -
With gentle lappings on the shoreline
Or the ocean's thundering roar!
Now sail boats out from Fowey
Fill the bay like butterflies -
Sun glinting on the water
White clouds and clear blue skies.
Llansalos Church stands sentinel
In folds of autumn gold
And the pathways at Pencarrow
Are most beauteous to behold.

Margaret A P Quinn

AS LIFE GOES BY

The sun may be shining, in the sky
People walking, running by
But nobody looks to see
Or even takes notice of me
I'm just a nothing in this world
A baby in my arms I've held
The smile, joys of life it brings
Like the early bird that sings
Each day goes on the same old way
The fears and feelings put at bay
A new birthday comes each year
With every new year brings good cheer
Death is a force that is too strong
But it reaches us all before too long
So do in life what you wish to do
Before your time runs out on you.

Patricia Jones

THE WINDOW

The window,
Plain and insignificant.
The dust curtain
Closing hour by hour.
Cracked from corner to corner,
Diffracting the light,
Creating patterns
On the splintered floorboards below;
The sun's rays entrapped in the grime.
The room empty,
Except for the shards of glass
Thrown from the window,
Ready to slash and spear unprotected feet.
Battered by the elements,
The wind screaming through the fragmented pane,
The window unable to bar its entry
Defunct and derelict,
In the abandoned room,
Of a shattered soul.

John Rye

MY SONNET

How could someone, so full of goodness and love,
Now become so full of hatred, and vain.
You were like a silvery star from above.
But, alas now causes me tears and pain.

A friend so precious like a sacred wish,
Around you, I felt in my element.
Your beauty remains, but love has vanished,
Like a glistening rose, who'd lost her scent.

The real you has gone, a shadow remains,
Just a reminiscence of an old friend.
Could it be I will see you smile again?
Will the continual frown never end?

The mystery of thee will never be solved,
The laughter and warmth turned heartless and cold.

Emma Warsop (13)

ISLAND SUNSET

The sky was a vision of riotous colour
Stretching out above the land.

Amazing hues of flame and orange
Mingled, flowed and fanned.

A patch of startling turquoise blue
Outlined against the drawing night

Was edged with brilliant silver tongues
Of outward thrusting light.

Merging blues and fiery reds
Formed pink and purpling bands

Crowned by feathery foaming clouds
Of softly floating strands.

Darkening skies pressed quickly down
Upon the glowing embers dim,

As the sunset's passing glory
Fell beneath horizon's rim.

Audrey Clifton

OBSESSION

Enraptured by an Aphrodite of pristine perfection,
Who usurped all and every other ardent deep affection.

Such that it became an obsession, a madness in the mind,
A longed-for fantasy which few can ever hope to find.

Abandoned everything, forced to renounce his former life,
Forsaking hearth, home, children, fond and faithful wife -

Infatuated beyond recall, to all else unseeing,
Committed to find one who had ensnared his very being.

So possessed was he by this unspent passion, flaming, rife,
Addiction was to encompass all his acolyte life,

For the spell cast was such naught else was there that he could do,
It worked its magic as he searched for one he thought he knew.

Throughout life, years more than three score and ten,
Courage undaunted, impossible for most other men.

Soon to become an illusion that the years would then fade,
For with time memory distorts that of which dreams are made -

Youth most vulnerable when passing through life's portals,
Always fallible like other poor simple mortals.

My span lost in one instant's unquenchable flame,
Travail of years wandering, asking always your name.

My strength slips away from this ephemeral life,
Surely for me was naught but toil, sorrow, and strife.

A faint luminosity heralds the dawn,
The veil from my eyes now seems suddenly torn -

Your loved face before me in radiant sight,
I reach out to touch you with resurging might -

The night turns to day, birds sing, joyous once more,
I'm with you dear heart, at last, forever more.

Death at the end has brought peace, bliss, blessed sweet rest,
In tender embrace close to your welcome warm breasts.

Laura Edwards

THE MILLENNIUM YEAR

Do we look forward or do we look back,
As this year draws to its close.
It started with such high hopes and dreams,
Where they are gone to, no one knows.

We start a rather special year,
As this ninety-nine one ends.
The year 2000 dawns today,
But we know not what it sends!

We long for health and love and peace,
That war shall be no more.
Let's all have faith and hope and trust,
As we open this new year's door.

This new year we shall see no more,
As we tread the millennium's soil.
Let's open our hearts and look ahead,
As through each day, we will toil.

Give both friend and foe our hand in trust,
Let's walk our way with hope.
Steps may be hard, the way be rough,
But with God's help, we shall cope.

A Cheek

HEAVEN

Is there a star for me in heaven?
Can I see it from the Earth?
Does it symbolise my goodness?
Does it signify my worth?
Is there a cloud for me in heaven?
Can I look down on the Earth?
Have I earned enough points
to have my own wings
or did I earn them at birth?
Can I fly amongst the angels
and the loved ones who before
ascended heavenwards
when their mortal forms
fell tragically in war?
Or when they descended into slumber
at the end of a long natural life?
But most of all
can I wait at the gates
when St Peter calls for my wife?

George Dale O'Cock

ONCE

Once a little boy
Now a sound fine man
But what of the in between?
Consider if you can

Once on the street
Drawn to a legendary gang
Safety amongst numbers
But the alarm bells never rang

Once enticed naive
Victim to the charm
This boy came of age
And with it came the harm

Once on the other side
Now a sound fine man
That now was the in between
And from it he had ran!

Ivan Sepp

JOEY

Joey had achieved his greatest ambition,
To become a circus clown, like his father.
He revelled in his work,
In applying his make-up, wig and red nose;
Donning his garish costume and shoes with upturned toes.
He liked the music as he entered the ring,
The applause as he left it;
The acrobatics and practical jokes,
With laughter and simulated tears;
And above all, the children,
Bouncing up and down on their seats,
Bright-eyed and excited.
Now, for the first time, he was reluctant to perform,
For his father was gravely ill
And would never appear with him again.
He felt desolate, but he braced himself
And as the music sounded he ran into the ring;
This time with feigned laughter and genuine tears.
He was following tradition. The show had to go on.

Dorothy K Springate

MILLENNIUM MADNESS

Millennium madness millennium gladness
At last the Dome and Big Wheel in place
The cost of all a real disgrace,
The price of going through the Dome
Enough to make one groan and groan
Going on the whole year through
Always wondering what next they will do
I expect a band with a drummer's drum
And a trumpet call must be done
They will ring tunes on church bells
They erected a clock in Tunbridge Wells
Restoration is done on Brighton Station
Wondered at by all the nation
Millennium madness, millennium gladness
The last day hard to get through
Depending what you want to do
It will be the longest day
Until you light your firework display
Stars shooting in the sky
With rockets whirling high
Millennium madness, millennium gladness
At last it's all come true
Except to say
      Happy New Year to you.

Ellen King

LOVE RE-AWAKENED

Was it a dream when first I saw your face?
The beauty in your eyes, it haunts me still,
and now that longing for another place,
where now you are, so far away, it will
remain with me for evermore.

Was it a dream when first I held your hand?
Wary you seemed of me, a stranger then,
but soon to share our thoughts, we talked, and
now I long to feel you near me once again.
Was it a fantasy?

No, it was real, just as the rising sun
which warms my heart, and melts away the pain
that I have felt, and now I have begun
to see the beauty of this world again.
This is reality,

I feel the softness of the falling rain
washing away the tears that fill my eyes.
Now they are gone, and love has come again.
It fills my heart with joy to realise
that you are there.

Winter has passed: no longer does the cold
sadden my soul with grief and loneliness,
for you are there, and all my thoughts unfold
into serenity and happiness
as I think of you.

John Hall

The Norfolk Coast

Soft, salty winds gently buffet
as in the distance a lone sail
breaks through the line of sea and sky.
Placid cattle up to their hocks
in the oozy mud, tails sweeping
away the rude pestering flies.
Far away the village windows
fired by the evening sun, sparkle.
The church spire points man heavenward
reminding of another world.
On the dunes sea holly jostles
with marram grass, samphire and thrift.
A rotting dinghy's gaunt bleached ribs
a pulpit for a raucous gull.
Puffy clouds kissed a carmine hue
herald the fast approaching night.

John J Allan

My Dream

The scene is set inside a place
That's hushed and quiet with humble grace
There lies a window just ahead
Through which a ray of light is shed
Before me stands a holy sight
And as the sun shines to my right
I turn my head to look that way
And then know why I'm here today
A glow picks out the gold and red
As it falls upon my loved one's head
His eyes look into mine and say,
It's here at last, 'Our Wedding Day'.

Carol Ann Urwin

THE DIET

I'm going on a diet, I'm starting it today
I have brought some cottage cheese and fruit to help me on my way
I'm going on a diet, I will be eating lots of fish
I will be finished with the chips and pies, for me it's grapefruit in a dish

I'm going on a diet, I will be running every night
I will do it in the darkness lest the neighbours get a fright.
I will be counting every calorie and counting all the fat
if I keep it up for long dear, I will need a smaller hat.

I will be full of fruit and veg you know, I will be full of yoghurt too
if I carry on like this for long I will be living on the loo.

I'm going on a diet, I was going to start today,
when I've had my steak and chips dear, I will start it straightaway.
I promise I will stick to it from the bottom of my heart,
can you pass the cream for this piece of apple tart?
I'm very fond of creamy cakes, sausages and chips
I will have to put them all away and just eat carrot sticks.

Perhaps I will start next Monday or Friday maybe best
or shall I start on Saturday? I will put it to the test.
I could start it after Christmas, or Easter can't be bad,
or maybe I won't bother, maybe it's a fad.
I don't need to go on a diet, I am just a little round
and no one will ever notice if I put on half a pound

So I'm not going on a diet and I'm not starting it today
so put away the crispbreads dear
I don't like them anyway.

Lynn Barry

MY DAY OUT

I went to Dymchurch,
had a lovely day out,
picked up some seashells,
as I wandered about.

The sea felt so warm,
as it lapped round My feet,
I was glad I had come,
to this peaceful retreat.

I called at Brock cottage,
to visit the girls,
heard all the gossip,
first Wendy's then Pearl's.

Saw some of Joan's paintings,
they were very good,
I can't paint myself,
but I do wish that I could.

Betty made the teas,
for each one of us there,
Peggy gave us all cakes,
Mine was an eclair.

We talked of things past,
Walked down Memory Lane,
and had such a great day,
we planned to do it again.

Now it's goodbye to Dymchurch,
no more will I roam,
until the next time,
Swanley, I'm on My way home.

Pamela Eckhardt

AT PEACE

The sound of gunfire filled the air
the smell of smoke was everywhere
No sleep no rest plagued by rats
forever wearing our hard tin hats
mud that sticks to clothes and boots
our feet rot away while the Jerry shoots
lost, afraid, confused in danger
I dare not show my fear and anger
death surrounds me along with pain
men drowned in mud, please God no rain
A letter sent from my dear mother
I read over and over for I have no other
I saw a Tommy his head blown away
my turn next so I ran astray
Deserter, traitor, the top brass cried
Home for Xmas, it was they that lied
So now I stand my blindfold ready
Before me the firing squad, their guns held steady
I feel a tear roll down my cheek
A sign of cowardice so I blink
Gunfire rips now through my body
Killed by friend and not by foe
At peace at last I'm free to go
So forget my name on your roll of honour
And cast white feathers to the wind
For I have been before a higher jury
And heaven knows I have not sinned.

R Biggs

HOMELESS CHRISTMAS

Sleeping in a cardboard box
Beneath the stars on hard, cold ground.
A few small luxuries make the box a home:
A sleeping bag and chocolate.
With others around in the drizzling rain,
Sitting in their cardboard worlds.
Thinking, dreaming, praying,
Hoping the comfort of summer soon comes,
Knowing December will bite first.
The drunk in the corner, gulping from bottles;
The youth with only a blanket,
Young but long past innocent;
The addict lying still,
Hallucinating a faraway dream of a bed.
The couple in one box, snuggling up for warmth;
All with a common goal that night,
Beneath the bright full moon -
To survive another sunset,
To face another dawn,
Only to perpetuate the cycle of poverty and pain.
Christmas lies a world apart,
With presents and joy nowhere here.
No Santa Claus or children's smiles
Or trifle or pudding or cake
Or turkey with all the trimmings.
They're fairy tales and myths for some,
Distant memories for others who now live
In those cardboard homes.

Alastair Wilkinson

THE FAMILY

Nancy was a novelist
Of wit and charm and humour
She also specialised in tease,
In gossip and in rumour

Pam married a scientist,
In his field uniquely skilled
Brave Tom loved girls and music
But was untimely killed

Diana wed a Guinness heir
A marriage doomed to fail -
She left him for the Fascist chief
And spent the war in jail

Unity adored her Fuhrer
And, when the war broke out
She tried to take her life, but lived
Through being strong and stout

Decca was a Communist
And ran away to fight
In the Spanish Civil War
Against the extreme Right

The youngest, Debo, now a Duchess,
Writes amusing books
Her beauty beats advancing years -
She still retains her looks.

I J Critchley

WONDERFUL WORLD

What a wonderful world it would be
To live in love and harmony
To love not hate, for peace not war,
To give and take, no fighting, no more,
Go hand in hand, take each day as it comes,
As we all grow older, from being young.
Enjoy your days, enjoy your dreams,
Don't look back at what could have been.
Look back with love, look back with pride,
For growing up can be a tough ride.
We age, we mellow, the years go so fast,
Look to the future, not the past.
All your goals, your dreams you've made,
Some come true, others fade.
Be happy, not sad, live life to the full
For God gave life to us all.

Angela Simpson

THE LUNAR MOON

If you look in the sky
In the early morning
you'll see a Lunar moon
is turning
Swiftly through the dark unseen
go back to sleep
and finish that dream
Cosmic dust is falling through
and causing a millennium flu
and not a bug that first was thought
and so a millennium tale was bought.

E M Ocock

AS AUTUMN FALLS

Farewell for now to summer skies
Welcome autumn's splendour,
As Mother Nature changes hue
Her coat she shall surrender.

From trees aflame her foliage spills
Stiff breezes help to shed,
Golden brown and russet tones
A carpet deep to tread.

Bring forth the autumn equinox
As night skies fall with haste,
Then in a cloak of stagnant mist
The dawn shall be encased.

Bonfires alight as sparkles flare
Upturned children's faces
Chestnuts hot on embers glow
A rocket skyward chases.

Willow brooms, All Hallows Eve,
The knock of trick or treat,
Pumpkin faces in lanterns glow
A toffee apple sweet.

As autumn now takes centre stage
With frost upon her wing
For winter soon will play her part
To stir the sleeping spring.

Angela Wornham

WHY I NEED TO WIN A HOLIDAY
IN UNDER 40 WORDS

Tesco's is
terrific
Waitrose is
a wow

But
I need an
adventure
and
I need it
now.

Safeway's is
safe
Marks does
Thai

But
I need to
get past Europe
before
I die.

Jane Glover

NEVER FORGOTTEN

A very sweet old lady
Miss Dolley was her name,
Whenever I called to see her,
She always was the same.

No one was more contented
In this busy world of ours,
Her great joy was her garden,
How she adored the flowers!

I will never forget dear Miss Dolley,
As I travel along Life's way,
I'll always remember to count my blessings,
As I know she did every day!

Bridget Hollman

A SOLDIER'S FATE

Steady beat
Marching feet
Banging drum
Time has come
Nerves drawn tight
No wrong or right
Wait for the sign
To advance in line
Into enemy fire
Across the wire
Ground to gain
Through the pain
Drawing breath
Close to death?
A soldier's fate
To watch and wait
Death as the end
To foe and friend
Remember the past
They won't be the last.

Tracy Enright

Why I'd Rather Have Toothache Than Be In Love

I n both there is much pain

L aconic that might seem
O nerous misery for sure
V ariable pain that's in store
E ventually a tooth can be pulled and be calmed

Y et with love there is no soothing balm
O nly hope for a future together
U ntil then abject misery forever.

Paul Clement

The Promise

I am in your heart, but you don't know me.
I love you, I respect you and leave you free.
So take care of what you think, say and do
For I always agree with you.
The power of love is very great
And so the power of hate!
Love is my divinity
Freedom is your humanity
Think Man
Face your responsibility!

Silva Rota-Wills

FANTASY LOVE

All I remember are scenes of places,
people holding empty faces.
But one held more than one can trace,
the sign of something extra in their grace.
The seasons, the weather and his face. Eyes with eternal space.
Moon and stars, lights, and you and your face.
There you were, here and there,
all over the place. Going here, going there, racing.
Turning and saying goodbye, we are pacing.
Wearing, what was he wearing?
Caught, caught in a trance so caring.
Does it go on into the night with the music?
Into the day with the transparent winds?
Does he remember or imagine the confusion
when the senses are closing in?
We got lost in some melody from the heavens,
I was wise to flee and turn away.
Unsurfaced was a world held at bay.
I dreamed, did he dream?
Past the nights, past the stars, past the world of his heart.
I starred in his favourite movie,
appearing with a romantic blanket to drape his life in.
We want to carry on, but there's no time that's ours to belong.
He could have said, could have done, but it was wrong.
I let it be, and be, it was gone . . .
Like the wind in the hands of God.

Heidi Welch

UNTITLED

You look at your life, it's not what it seems,
Things do not turn out, like they do in your dreams.
But if you look deep enough, I'm sure you can find
A person who's loving, and caring, and kind.
One who is faithful, honest and true,
One who's one thought, is only for you.
So one thing to look for, right from the start,
Is not what they look like, but what's in the heart.
They may not be perfect, and have some bad ways,
But they will protect you, throughout all your days.
They have no ego, their first thought is you,
They'll back you up, whatever you do.
So the one thing to remember, when you next look,
Is don't judge the cover, in what's inside the book.

B G Standen

AS THE MINUTES PASS

As the minutes pass, my prayers continue upwards,
In meditation and with faith I hold you ever near.
Asking only for strength and guidance for the coming year,
Tranquillity will come, and help will surely follow
'As the minutes pass'.
Guidance not from Earthly things, but never-ending from afar.
Holding hands on high, joining hands in silent prayers,
Answers will come, believe just a little more,
The peace that follows will be abundant . . .
              'As the minutes pass'.

Liz Dicken

GINGER

Through the frosted window
I see a wondrous sight,
This sighting only happens
In the darkness of the night.

I sense there's someone's watching
I tingle with delight,
For then I see two emerald eyes,
Twinkling, oh so bright.

There he is, it's Ginger,
He visits from above,
He greets me each and every day,
This puss I really love.

He looks so proud and dapper,
With his fur so nicely groomed,
He smiles at me and winks an eye,
With cuddles soon resumed.

He rolls about from side to side,
Looks mischievous, with glee,
I know this daily ritual,
He wants to share my tea.

Eventually I do succumb,
And feed him this and that,
He meows at me with begging tone,
He is a hungry cat!

Then it's bedtime, soon enough,
It's nice to rest my head,
But who is that upon my feet?
It's Ginger on the bed.

Connie Garrard

THE OLD OAK

He had seen many a year come and go
Warm sunny days and winter snow
The leaves on his branches have all been spent
Now he is old and his back is bent.

He remembers the days when upright he stood
With other young trees deep in the wood
Small birds built their nest safe in his leaves
In autumn the squirrels on acorns would feed.

Flowing nearby was a small, clear stream
Into it bright rays of sunshine would beam
Many's the time autumn winds blew around
Then gently his leaves would float down to the ground.
Nothing disturbed this peaceful place
Life went on at a gentle pace.

But times changed in the tranquil wood
A pathway was built where the trees once stood
So now all of this seems a long time ago
The old tree stands alone at the side of a road.

D Parsons

LOVE IS . . .

Love is like the blooming rose,
That delicately grows and grows.
That blossoms when two hearts are fused,
And never is the bond abused.

That strives to reach the highest skies,
When someone sought hovers nearby.
That reddens at the slightest flirt,
No matter if vague or overt.

That aches and wilts when hope is dead,
And inward bends her sullen head.
That mourns so when she cannot hear,
The call of love that once was near.

As sure as roses meet their doom,
New love returns once more to bloom.

Katie Rogers

PILGRIM FATHERS

As did the Pilgrim Fathers journey thus
Placing faith and hope and binding trust
Following a path of pain and need
Reaping harvests of plenty, against adversity and greed

Has not their stories been timelessly told
Like a beacon to guide us through years, new and old
Are we so different I ask myself true?
Battling for our tomorrow's, in each deed that we do

Should we not live in this hour now?
For our tomorrow's may be lost to us somehow
Be of courage know of pain
Footsteps washed by eternal rain

Hold on to your dreams that join two loving souls
Like a slither of cobwebs that encircles you whole
For each minute grain of love is gathered in the dust
To blow somewhere . . . but be nowhere

We know this is true and just
Joining pilgrims now at last
Turning the days into future
And the future into past

Susan Goldsmith

UNTITLED

Today upon a bus, I saw a lovely girl with golden hair,
I envied her, she seemed so gay, and wished I were as fair.
When suddenly she rose to leave, I saw her hobble down the aisle,
She had one foot and wore a crutch, but as she passed she smiled.
Oh God, forgive me when I whine.
I have two feet . . . the world is mine!

Then I stopped to buy some sweets
The lad who served had such charm, I talked with him.
He said to me, 'It's nice to talk to folk like you.
You see,' he said, 'I'm blind!'
Oh God, forgive me when I whine.
I have two eyes . . . the world is mine!

Walking down the street I saw a child with eyes of blue.
He stood and watched the others play.
It seemed he knew not what to do.
I stopped a moment, then I said, 'Why don't you join
                                        the others, dear?'
He looked ahead, without a word, and then I knew he could not hear.
Oh God, forgive me when I whine.
I have two ears . . . the world is mine!

With feet to take me where I'd go
With eyes to see the sunset glow
With ears to hear what I would know.
Oh God forgive me when I whine.
I'm blessed indeed. The world is mine.

Patricia Algar-Jones

HOLLY

Those little hands, tiny feet,
Impish smile - oh so sweet!
Radiating hope and love,
Were you plucked from heaven above?
'Baby Holly' your smile so bright
Dimmed only by the fall of night.
Time now for peaceful sleep,
Cry not little one - do not weep,
Someone will be there at the break of day
To smooth and wipe those tears away.

Strong hands to guide you through the years
May their strength abound, as dawn appears.
As then carried home for rest
Hear bird songs from their cosy nest.
Fledglings, before first they flew
In need of love, as are you.
Then to toddle on summer days
Enjoying love and words of praise.
We will watch you 'Little Star',
To see you're loved as others are.

'Little Holly', how you will grow,
Forming ideas of your own.
Smelling roses in the park,
Their beauty matched by your eyes so dark.
Raven hair and dark brown eyes,
Taking us all by surprise.
Pray you have a life that's good
And blossom into womanhood.
To look back on those younger years,
With no sorrow and no fears,
And we that love you, with glad sighs
Can brush a tear from happy eyes.

Bob Lock

LIFE

I'll live my life to the full
This will start when I leave school
I'll earn some money, improve my life
Hopefully I will become someone's wife

Go on holiday, see the sights
Like Las Vegas with its lights
See my friends, keep in touch
With the ones I care for very much

As for children, two will do
With regular trips to the zoo
As I did with my family
Who made me who I am originally

As for life now it's sometimes unfair
As I was born with dark hair
If I had a wish that would come true
I would like to be fair and five-foot two!

Whatever happens in life, I give my best
Nothing else matters, so sod the rest!

Debra Burchell

AUTUMN

Autumn the Painter has been working anew
With his colourful palette of myriad hue
From palest of yellow through golden to red
Tenderly putting the summer to bed
This pageant of beauty makes my heart sing
and takes me through winter
Till I welcome the spring.

Millie Malcolm

UNTITLED

O' windmill looking down,
Why do you wear such a frown?
Those fine woven sails, so limp and sad,
Is it the weather, that has been so bad?
No stone turning, to grind the meal,
Is it worry, and really how you feel?
If you are no use, you are no good at all,
That's obvious, where your back's against the wall.
Will you survive, if you can't give
That service to others, that they might live?
What a grind, some wit would say,
Amused, by your sense of decay.
Just a mocking retort, you would be better left on the shelf,
No concern, for that, once proud, erect self.
No regard, for the things you have done,
His thoughts, for only one.
What a history, you have gathered in your arms,
With pride and pleasure, showing your charms.
Rapturous cries, of wonder and awe,
Mingling, with shouts of 'Encore, encore.'
Your memories, never to cherish anymore,
Just fading away, for evermore.
No longer, will you grace the scene,
You will be just what they call, a 'has-been'.
The evolution of this world, is the death of thee,
Not even an epitaph, you see.

Bruce Dann

NOLEEN'S BLUES

In sleepless dreams I wander,
Through the passages of my mind.
Your name echoes round every corner that I take.
Though I run from you,
The thought of you engulfs my senses,
And leaves me reeling in the surf,
Of my wild seas,
The watery desert of insomnia.
I close my eyes,
But I cannot blind myself from your image,
Which imprints on my retina,
More vividly than the brightest sun.
I run to the window and peer outside.
And by the moon shining down on me,
I look out for you,
And picture you standing in the shadows of my room.
But as liquid you flow from me,
Leaving me to ponder your memory,
Like a tragic flower.

Dave Wingfield

MORNING DEW

The sun has come out
Plants droop from their spouts,
It is so bright, what a sight!
The sparkle from the morning light
The still grass is like cracked glass
Starting to move from the cold night.
The frost slowly melts away
For it is a brand new day
Glistening in the sunshine
Everything is well, everything is fine.

Lawrence Moore (12)

THE ANCIENT ONE

Through the mists of time the warrior came,
riding the stallion black as night,
evoked by one who called his name,
ready again to stand and fight.

Ancient leather creaked as they sped,
his mighty sword swung at his side,
a mystic aura round his head,
moon through the trees his only guide.

All through the night they galloped on,
thunder of hooves shaking the ground,
stopping at last, they stood upon
the fated spot, never a sound.

Once more he mounted, sword in hand,
with head held high, haughty and proud,
striking terror across the land,
no man dare speak his name aloud.

Fury unleashed, he slew them all
excepting one, who hid from sight,
knew he dwelt in Valhalla's Hall,
returning there before the light.

The mighty warrior gave a yell,
turned his horse and quickened his pace,
leaving behind the scene from hell,
vanished once more without a trace.

A Odger

MEMORIES

I remember winds blow
Sitting, watching the rivers flow.

I remember birds in flight
Howling winds in the dead of the night.

I remember pouring rains
Fast cars and high speed trains.

I remember laughing loud
And scoring the goal that made me proud.

I remember golden sands
Falling gently between my hands.

I remember the sunshine
Feeling sick and feeling fine.

I remember my only friend
And watching his life come to an end.

I remember throwing it all away
And still regretting it to this very day.

And drinking whisky from my favourite cup
And lying back and giving up.

Darren Abbott

SEEKING SIGNS OF SEASONS NEW . . .

Old leaves scrunch beneath my feet
as I stride through wooded glade.
Seeking signs of seasons new,
in scented dappled glade.

Could I ever tire, of chestnuts' regal spires
or birches' silver hue -
where bluebells now shimmer anew?

Above my head, squirrel chatters
in his mischievous way -
at magpies who natter, having their say!

Hedgehog, in this secret place
where Queen Anne flaunts her white lace,
doesn't change his pace, as I step lightly by.
Flirting, morning breeze shares my contented sigh . . .!

Joanne Manning

ICEBERG

The sound of her breath
as she sweeps the fractured sky
the ice in her veins
breaks loose when I cry;

The water in which she swims
is deadly and tastes of salt
the religion in her eyes, burns
as her reigns are trapped and caught;

Her body is like a bridge
between the land and me
arched in perfect beauty
across a stormy sea.

She rises with the squall
and falls in the calm
lying in her icy vales
I feel no threat of harm.

Bill Talbott

FROM CHAOS TO CHAOS

Pure golden light did flood the Eastern sky
Blessing the world with warmth of dawn
Slowly as if the burning disk felt shy
Observing her children forlorn.

Exhausted, unworshipped she wept in vain
Cruel offspring ignoring her grief,
Damned for crimes of nourishing life
Vengeful on the ungrateful thief.

Absorbing life she once proudly suckled
Her glory refuelled by the Earth,
Eternal flames flashed and flickered afresh
With miraculous blessed re-birth.

Followers of faith cursed Gods in despair,
Heaven's rusty gates neglected.
Impatient Hell waited hungry for strays
Their crops from virtue protected.

Happiness rejoiced in the fiery core
Freed planets danced glad with the star
Blessed for curing the celestial plague
Rocks settled to peace spread afar.

Infernal laughter ripped with shocking gasp
When no purpose employed her light
Never to share her warmth with life again
Ran screaming to darkness in fright.

Cressida Allen

REMEMBER VERY LONG AGO

Remember childhood days
Remember childhood ways,
Reading comics every week
Playing the game of hide and seek.
After Sunday School singing hymns of praise
And on Monday morning back to school again,
Being taught arithmetic of pounds, shillings and pence
To use your brains to add up and use your common sense -
There were no computers or ready-reckoners then at all
Now they have them to use in nearly every school.
Remember being in the choir and singing out of tune
And learning the plus time-tables in the school room;
Going out to play bat and ball was much more fun.
Than taking part in the school team to run
Taking part in school sport's day you had to be quick
It was much better running down the street with a hoop and stick.
Remember being kept home from school with mumps, measles
                                   or chickenpox,
And putting numbers on the path for the jumping game of hop-scotch.
Remember playing ring-a-ring of roses with girls and boys
And standing round the bonfire with fireworks that made a loud noise
Remember going to the park to get on the swing to sway
And going to the Sunday School outing to the seaside for the day.
Remember going to the tuck-shop to buy a pennyworth of sweets
Like liquorice allsorts, chocolate buttons, milk gums, sherbet dabs
                                   so many treats.
A lot of things in life have changed now, this we all know
And so of course do you remember all this happened very long ago?

Kay Downing

BETRAYAL

Softly, as I survey your sleeping form
And reflect on the troubles recently born
How to imagine life without you
And all the wonderful things you do
To think that I could have caused such pain
By stupidly straying again and again
Forgetting so easily the joys we shared
And letting myself get so ensnared
By seeking the youth and glamour displayed
And however you put it just getting laid
How could I casually betray your trust
And given in easily to moments of lust
When at last discovered, confessions came
But things were never quite the same
Now time has passed and anger spent
Our vows renewed and really meant
God made women to forgive
Otherwise, how could I live

B Chandler

THE SEARCH

I followed the path through the wood
And quickly lost sight of the town.
Unsure of where I was going
Winding tracks led me on and down.

I passed squirrels dancing in trees
And a fox chasing his playmate.
Blue tits flew 'round the grand old oak.
So much to see - I couldn't wait.

The path led me on to the lake.
Over the bridge my feet carried me.
I was in search of the old house,
Abandoned to the wild ivy.

I looked in vain for my desire -
A very rare and tiny plant.
Like a fairy in the garden.
To say that I'd seen one - I can't!

Barbara Pearce

PEACE

Be at peace, oh my soul
from the troubles that surround thee,
for they are but the passage of time
and they cannot touch thee.

Reach out with thine hands to the tangible things of God.
Seek with thine eyes for His truth and beauty.
Believe and trust in Him who truly cares,
He who took your heavy burden of sin
and gave you freedom and life.

Look to the heavens on a summer's day
See the calmness, the tranquillity and
Be at peace, oh my soul.

Isabel Davitt

THE GIFT OF THE MAGI

In the east, travellers from afar,
Are seen following a shiny star,
Some say they are kings
Others - wise men,
We know only one thing
There are three of them.
First, there's Casper the leader of them all,
Balthazar and Melchoir
Who heard the spiritual call.
'Let's follow' began Casper,
'The star that God has made,
For if we do we're sure to find
The virgin with her babe.'

Finally, they found the place
Where the infant Jesus lay.
They bowed their heads and worshipped him,
Then began to pray.
Once they had paid him homage,
They told people what had come.
The most precious person that had ever lived,
God's precious son.

And so the story that is told
Of what the three men saw,
Tells us simply to believe
And Christmas comes once more.

Elizabeth Meehan

CAT ON THE DOORSTEP

I ventured out to sniff the air
And give my catty friends a stare,
But I don't want to sit all night
On this cold step till morning light.

When I was young it was okay
To be put out at close of day,
But now I'm old, rheumatic too,
I'd rather be indoors with you.

It gets so cold from 2 - 5
Amazing that I stay alive!
My fur's all damp, my whiskers too -
I'd like to come indoors with you.

The dog's tucked up, you've said 'Goodnight,'
You've locked the door, switched off the light,
And now you've both gone up to bed,
And left me on the step instead.

I would so love to be in there
To snooze upon a comfy chair.

So please, before you lock me out
Remember this - without a doubt,
In daylight, I do like to roam,
At night, I want to stay at home.

Beryl Richardson

IN THE COMPANY OF ANGELS

(For Nicola)

An angel landed by her side
to take to Heaven a poorly child
to wake her from the dream of life
and enter her into Paradise
Carry her unto Heaven's gate
where there is no pain and peace awaits

Angels welcome her blessed soul
into the kingdom of divine love
to where you can never be old
Hope springs eternal and God is love
for no life is ever in vain
Because the spirit shall rise again

In the company of angels
she'll dance till the day she'll be reborn
till then a guardian angel
Sheltering someone safe from the storm
sing out your praises to the sky
for your guardian angel's close by

For even in the darkest night
when doubt appears and the spirit fades
Behold and you will see the light
there is no reason to be afraid
Christ is with us all our days till fate brings
the conclusion of the system of things

S P Chesterman

A PROMISE TO KEEP

The girl closed her eyes
And whispered in prayer
She wished he was beside her
And not over there

The parting was bitter
Bad things had been said
She could not kiss him goodbye
Lots of tears had been shed

He did not have to go
His reason was loyalty
In full uniform
He looked just like royalty

In the air raid shelter
She sat full of fear
Her hands clasping her stomach
Protecting the baby so dear

If he returned safe and sound
The promise she made
Was to love him forever
The rest of her days

Fifty years later
She at last said goodbye
To her hero the soldier
Who returned to her side

Her promise she kept
And loved him forever
The war had not parted them
They had grown old together.

Angela Eames

ONE THING PUZZLES ME

There are brilliant men in the world these days
Who can change our lives in many ways
We have radio and hi-fi too
And television at home to view

Men go in rockets to outer space
With plastic surgery they can mould a new face
They've built a new tunnel miles under the sea
How the workmen kept dry is a mystery to me

The micro dot the eye can't see
The phone to keep in touch with my family
Men can jump from the sky down to earth
From a test tube now can women give birth

There are planes that beat the speed of sound
Oil pumped from the sea and underground
Computers now to take the strain
And motorways to beat the train

Submarines stay weeks on the seabed
Such marvellous things of which I've read
But pardon me for being so bold
Why can't they cure the common cold?

E M Harvey

MILLENNIUM

The noise on the street is so loud,
Everywhere you look there is a crowd.
People laughing, having fun,
A new millennium has begun.
The noise from houses fills the air,
And fireworks explode from everywhere.
Bangs and smoke, laughter and cheer,
Brought about by wine and beer.
'Happy New Year' yells a voice through the din,
Say goodbye to '99 it's gone in the bin.
Now the day slowly begins to break,
The colours are spectacular and really awake,
The colours are electric, so too is the crowd,
With the new dawn approaching, so too is a cloud.
What will this dawn hold for those all around,
I stand and wonder as I wait in this crowd,
I watched the sun as it rose from the ground,
The world has rejoiced, and now we sleep sound.

Claire Russell (16)

THIS APRIL MORNING

This April morning
a *swoosh* of sound
above my head.
A flight of birds
in gracious symmetry,
one beautiful movement,
almost one thought.

Karen Monaghan

ORION 3

I live on a planet, it's called Orion 3,
We make our own breakfast and we make
our own tea.
Our planet is a square one, or sometimes
even round,
We live on Orion 3, we never hear a sound.

Maybe it's deserted, maybe it's not there,
No one seems to notice, no one seems to care.
We're near to another planet, it's called Orion 4,
But no one ever likes to go there, anymore.

We love our little planet and all its habitat,
Oh, and I forgot to mention there are some
dogs and cats.
There's even an Orion 5, next to number 4,
But no one seems to live in our solar system,
anymore.

Ben Hughes (11)

SUNBURST

Sunshine explodes through the window,
On a kingdom of tables and chairs,
And it traces an intricate pattern,
With a subtle prismatic stare.

It bounces off bottles and glasses,
Sets fire to the barmaid's hair,
Then mirrors the minds of the strangers,
Till those eyes once so distant are near.

Burnt-black sits a cat in its corner,
Mesmerised by the flaming sun,
While the milk turns blood-red in her saucer,
Does she dream? Does she yearn to be young?

In a haze sunlight strains to the window,
Like a song that was haunting too long,
Yet the ghost of its gaze still lingers,
Where life's jigsaw of colours began.

Ron Ayliffe

IN LOVING MEMORY

When at night I cannot sleep
Into dreams I wish to peep.
Dreams of memories long ago
When life was travelling to and fro.
Now that togetherness has come to pass
When a loved one is resting under grass.
Years too have so much flown
And life is different living on alone,
Then joy and happiness again behold
When loving family is there to unfold.
Little ones playing joyfully around
Help the tears of loss to abound.
Life goes on whatever is the great gap,
It is not a rehearsal but to be lived between each nap.

Iris E Weller

THINKING OF YOU

Each time I pass by the old fighter base,
I feel so sad inside
My thoughts race back to the war-torn years
And the tragic way you died.

So many died upon the ground
Even more up in the sky,
But for your nerve and fortitude
I too, would have surely died.

I stand here, in this British field
And think of secrets it could yield,
From around the world they came to us
To fight day and night without a fuss.

Is that the sound of a Hurricane I hear
With a Spitfire at its side?
No! It's neither of these
It's just the wind playing with my mind.

I look around in this New Age
At youngsters in their prime,
You were once as they are now
But died before your time.

Time is a great healer they do say,
But that's not entirely true,
Not one day passes by
That I fail to think of you.

The debt we owe can never be paid
Those words have been written before,
To you men and women of the RAF
I'll remember you evermore.

John H Israel

I FELL IN LOVE WITH AN MP

I fell in love with an MP
It was love at first sight
He walked towards me
With a cup of tea

On this special night
I went to a meeting
Our eyes met across a crowded room
It wasn't long before we dated
Hugging and kissing under the moon

He sensed my life was so bad
He realised I had been beaten by my Dad
His heart went out to me
Only wanting to see
How happy I could be
He made me laugh
He made me cry
When I told him I could not read or write

My father is the reason why
He sent me to school of a night
Telling me I was doing well
Doing alright
My life is not so much a hell
As I've learnt to write and spell
I fell in love with an MP
Now we are so in love
He wants to marry me

Barbara Towes

FAIRIES

Do you believe in fairies
Do you believe they exist?
Folk say they have seen fairies
Have they been looking through a mist?
Do you believe in fairies
Do you believe they are real?
Have you seen a fairy
Or several dancing a reel?
Do you believe they are 'a load of old hat'
Or just for story appeal?
What of the fairy ring on your lawn
A circle so green and so round
How do you think it got there
Silently with no sound?
To those who say they have seen them
It is a privilege it is true
Have you seen a fairy?
Has one revealed itself to you?

Evelyn A Evans

SPRING INTO SPRING

Spring is bursting, winter has met with death
Yellow fluffy chicks take their first breath
Pretty red and pink tulips sway without a care
Yellow trumpets breeze in the spring air
Shimmering in the dew, fields of emerald green
Baby lambs frolic - a sight to be seen

Birds twittering their spring songs
Busy gardeners sorting right and wrongs
Seeds to be sown, bulbs turn to flower
Blazes of colour, trees, buds in full power
Children playing in boots 'twere muddy
Spring air refreshes, faces glow ruddy

So mild, fresh, this vibrant season
Not hot, nor cold, no germs, no reason
Could it not last all year round
No scorchers, hailstones, no snow to be found
Enjoy each season and stand the heat
Spring soon comes around - a refreshing treat.

Hazel Smith

LITTLE BUNNY

There was a little bunny
Who was very quiet and shy
The other bunnies would always tease
And make poor bunny cry.

One day this little bunny
Was hopping over the hill
She saw the farmer with a great big gun
'Oh no! He is out for the kill!'

Very scared was little bunny
But she knew it was down to her
To get back quick and warn the rest
And save all bunnies fur.

All of the little bunnies
Take shelter 'till the farmer's gone
And what did they all learn from this?
That to tease little bunny was wrong!

Sarah Louise White

THE ROMAN LIGHTHOUSE AT DOVER

The Romans built you in their ancient time,
A light to guide the galleys into port,
To stand like some still sentry on the cliff,
While in the town below they made their fort.

Long after all the Legions left these shores,
Until the Normans built a castle here,
You stood through all the bleak and darkest age,
And watched the town where people lived in fear.

The years went by, along with kings and queens,
Until it seemed the darker times were past,
From here the trading ships set sail for France,
A thriving town and port was growing fast.

King Henry Eight came to the port in pomp,
To Field of Cloth of Gold he sailed abroad,
You saw Spain's great Armada in defeat,
And watched King Charles's monarchy restored.

When England's realm was threatened yet again,
You saw great battles rage across the Strait,
When her flotillas braved Zeebrugge's hell,
And Dover found new fame as Freedom's Gate.

From clifftop perch you saw Luftwaffe's might
Defeated by a brave and gallant few,
When shells and bombs of hate rained on the town,
Until a gentle peace returned anew.

Your light no longer shines above the town,
The lonely gulls have made a refuge here,
Yet still you stand, reminder of the past,
And symbol of our freedom held so dear.

Geoffrey Elgar

THE SEASIDE

I like to be at the seaside
Wherever the seaside may be,
Blackpool or Bognor or Brighton
Or Bexhill by the Sea.

It's nice to be at the seaside,
I don't mind if it's calm or it's rough,
The tides are always changing
Of its moods I can't get enough.

To walk down the Prom on a nice sunny day,
Or stride, barefoot across sand,
Or paddle on the edge of the water
It's refreshing and feels really grand.

There are plenty of shops at the seaside
That sell everything you require,
Sun hats, beach balls and cooling ice-cream,
Even candyfloss, if you desire.

I like to sit in a shelter
And shade myself from the sun,
Or be shielded from a wintry breeze
With a flask of hot tea and a bun.

So take yourself off to the seaside
Anytime when you're feeling low,
Take on board the joy of the crowds there
As you watch all the tides ebb and flow.

Margaret Tindale

PROGRESS . . .

Once, keen young lads kicked a football about here
on this turf that was soft, green and muddy.
Sporting shirts washed by Persil mums but soon
besmirched by their sons, with faces all ruddy.

And knobbly knees often came to grief as the throng
pressed forward with speed to the goal, but when
Success came to those who put no foot wrong,
their joy was immense, and they grew fit and strong.

Today, there are great concrete slabs and breeze blocks,
since the Council decreed a bulldozer should call.
And very soon now another Lego town will be found
with identical streets that go round and round.

Elaine Hunt

PERSPECTIVE

While others yearn the future to foresee,
It's to the past that I'd my steps retrace:
Reclining by the Sea of Galilee
Two thousand years ago I'd seek a place;
Hearing first hand the words that Jesus spoke,
The Gospels' truth I'd know with certitude
Nor doubt five loaves in myriad pieces broke
Could serve to feed a hungry multitude.
Miraculous deeds men's minds may mystify,
But yet o'er time and space they would hold sway,
The seeds Christ sowed are slow to fructify:
In sight of God a millennium's but a day.
Ten centuries are such a little span,
'Tis 50 million since the world began!

Aubrey Woolman

SUSSEX

Kipling's and Belloc's immortal verse
Has left little more to be said
In praise of Sussex, my haven, my home,
Where I was born and bred.
Yet my spirit soars in wordless praise
O'er the sweeping slopes of her Downs,
Which shelter the picturesque villages
And ancient, historical towns.

'Tween hedgerowed fields and bluebell woods,
Down her wandering, leafy lanes,
My wanderlust is cooled and healed,
So here I would remain
And breathe the fragrance of the pines,
And taste the briny breeze,
And dream my dreams by her drifting streams,
Which meander down to the seas.

On her towering cliffs which guard the coast,
My soul can stretch and grow;
And though time and tide the shore may change,
Nought changes the peace I know.
For as fishing boats find harbour here
From the stormy sea's wild strife,
So here I've found my harbour from
The stress and strain of life.

So Sussex is where I'll live and die
Like my father and mother before,
And I'll sing the praise to the end of my days
Of my haven by the shore.

Jean M Warren

WONDERFUL WEDNESDAY

On Monday morn at the crack of dawn my talking clock shrieks 'Time'
It watches not the weather-cock so does so wet or fine
I expose my mitt to silence it and punch the button 'Snooze'
For at 6/03 with bonhomie I do not exactly ooze
But the gentle hum from the spinning drum soporific in extreme
Soothes me back to sleep (without counting sheep) and my wild,
                                          erotic dream
While knickers, shirts and boxer shorts in sweet abandon doth cavort.
I awake with a start and fall apart as out of bed I flop
When the on/off wire on my washer-drier brings the machine to a
                                          scrunching stop.
With shaky legs and a bag of pegs, be it frosty, windy, fine,
Like a flagship decked for a homebound stretch pegged clothes
                                          festoon the line.
Then, the kitchen, stairs and dining room are attacked with Hoover
                                    duster, polish broom,
While bathroom, bedrooms, landing, hall and other chores are
                                    Tuesday's haul.
Yes - weekdays from hell are the first two of the week with the house
                          pristine clean - but my nerves up the creek!

But

Wednesday, oh Wednesday - what wondrous bliss, I'm cheerfully alert
                                  at the sun's first kiss.
Then down the stairs in leaps and bounds for a gentle jog as the
                                  coffee's ground
The Daily Mail - front to back - while gulping coffee, hot and black
A full English breakfast soothing my belly as I cosily watch Kilroy
                                      on the telly!

Then lounging around the whole house as I please for 'Wednesday
                          sweet Wednesday' is my day of ease.
A leisurely toilet, a shave and a shower as the talking clock calls the
                                  mid-day hour
To cook - or not to cook - thinks I. Oh no! I've better fish to fry
So to the golf club off I sally, car radio blaring! 'Tin Pan Alley!'

A round, a pint, a three-course lunch putting the world to rights with
a friendly bunch.
Then home to tea and hot cross bun and the collie out for his
evening run
At 6 a G and T and then all the soaps until News at Ten
The late night film (they're usually 'suggestive') with a large mug of
Horlicks and chocolate digestives
As I climb the stairs in search of sleep I can easily put up with the
rest of the week!

John Elias

MY LAST HOUR

A waterfall of dreams
In my last trembling hour
Is cast about me.

My favourite tree of autumn
Leaves have shed their cloak
And laid it o'er me.

A Heaven full of stars, sad
Twinkling, whispering,
Shine down upon me.

The echo of a plaintive note
From some old violin
Is searching for me.

But I shall leave them all behind
For they are memories;
And take with me,

A waterfall of dreams,
My trembling hour, and *you*,
Whom I love so dearly.

Ann Safe

LONG YEARS AGO

Long years ago
I met the man of my dreams,
I was not free, one didn't break a vow,
The memory still lives with me -
He was tall, gracious as a prince,
With courtesy and charm
Taking my stole, to carry over his arm,
There was mutual attraction and love
As never before, to adore!
I had a special red dress
We dined at the famous Hungarian Restaurant,
I was thrilled!
The then Prince of Wales, dining at the next table
With one of his lady loves.
The orchestra played, and we danced,
Heart to heart, the violinist especially to me,
At our table I was enthralled,
As a princess - I confess
I still feel love
Unspoken, so for months
Then parting - just a wonderful memory -
And one still dreams - I am 97!

Madeline Chase

BUTTERFLY CLOUDS

Children, come dance to a melody sweet
Unheard in your eggshell hideaways:
Skip, tiny or little or bigger feet
Into the ballroom of the sky . . .
Choosing butterfly clouds as partners
For if they stumble you will not cry.

Suzette Childeroy Compton

COCKNEY PRIDE

Not all the panoramic scenes
Of distant lands
Can ever replace the sight
Of London's river
In the dusky twilight.
For as the last lingering afterglow
Of sunset, fades in the west
One by one the city dons
Her multi-coloured gems
Which come a'winking.
While high against the skyline
St Paul's great dome stands sentinel
And rules the lapping water
Hushed
From its daily trafficking.

Marion P Webb

CARING

When someone's ill and needs a friend
Be sure that you are there
When old and frail they need to know
They have someone to care
You say you're much too busy
So many things to do
But sometimes in the future
Just think, it could be you
Weak and tired and lonely too
The days and nights so long
Then you'll regret not being there
When you were well and strong

Cathie Bridger

Now I'm 13

It's my birthday today,
But mum says there's no time to lay.
She says I have to help do some jobs . . .
Quick, get out the mops.
Wash up the dishes, tidy my room,
Clean up the kitchen with the dirty old broom.
Make every single untidy bed,
Throw out my old bear named Ted.
Clean the windows until they shine,
Wash all the mirrors except for mine.
Mow up and down the lawn,
Throw out all my clothes that are torn.
Weed every muddy flower bed,
Till you can see all the flowers of red.
While mum sits reading a book,
Every now and again she takes a look.
Now I wish I wasn't turning thirteen -
I wake up - thank goodness it was only a dream!

Jessica Padgham

Thoughts Of You

Thoughts of you, your smiling face
Return me to a happier place
When we were young and we were free
So long ago eternity

And such was life a forgotten place
With love reflected in your face
The time you had was just for me
A glance for all the world to see

But time goes on not backward face
Perhaps on to a better place
If this is so I know for me
With you it will most surely be

I P Cook

A GRAND LADY

She's not so young
But not that old
Gentle and kind
With a heart of gold
She has smiling eyes
Hair touched with grey
Eager to help in any way
She isn't fat
But not that thin
Careful with dress
Neat, tidy and trim
Her pace is steady
But rather slow
She gives a kind word
Wherever she goes
With rosy cheeks
And smiling lips
She gives advice
And many a tip
With time and love
For the family
Grandma
Whoever else could she be!

Dorothy Durrant

THE MOBILE

Have you noticed how men who work with wood
Are three-dimensional, not close and thin,
Both faces blank as paper is, or tin,
But with qualities of understanding? These
They have learned from working the patient trees.

Men were stacking wood in an open shed
Beside the line: watched from the train
More beautiful than dancers. After rain
Grass was jewel-bright, the woodshed gold,
Sun-painted dark inside, and in their hold
Nodding planks were brush-strokes on the shade.
The little figures, toys of tissue nerves,
Appeared to dangle from the gilded curves,
Bringing to mind a mobile, craftsman-made,
Seen recently in town, a lovely thing,
Compact and poised and virile as a spring.

The train moved on for ever but the scene,
Like Wordsworth's dancing daffodils, I keep
For pleasure waking or when near asleep:
The gold, the umbered dark, the sparkling green
With painted figures turning to and fro
To every breath of summer's gentle touch,
Swaying, saying then,
'Men do not work with wood so much, so much
As wood with men, with men.'

Joan Bidwell

THE CANADIAN - SEPTEMBER 1941

If you forget my address in your book,
Or chance to hit upon it with a smile,
Yet will I hold the memory of your look
And memory will linger there awhile.

The scent of pine woods in your conversation,
The crossword puzzle that we nearly solved,
The fun we had, the rising sense of courage
That our new friendship held like veins of gold.

A fragile, unnamed beauty grew between us -
A rainbow-coloured bubble on a pipe;
All tremblingly we tossed it on our laughter,
The shadow thoughts of war were hidden quite.

Even the 'station tea' could not destroy it,
I think I saw it shining in your eyes.
You asked my name and it came trembling nearer
And I was like a 'watcher of the skies.'

I hesitantly offered you the money,
But you declined and said 'The hat's on me!'
It burned my tongue, but even this was funny;
There was such comfort in your company.

And leaving you was not a bit like parting,
'I shall be seeing you again' you said;
And I went dreaming on my lonely journey,
The shining bubble floating on ahead.

Marion B Alford

GOD'S WONDERFUL WORLD

The wonderful world of God is here
All about us wherever we look
We never have to shed a tear
For beauty shines forth as from out of a book.

A radiant sunrise in the morning
A vivid sunset on the sea at night,
No need to worry about a shepherd's warning
The sky is filled with an incandescent light.

A mountainside filled with dazzling snow
A clear blue lake reflecting the sky.
There are beautiful things we'll never know
But just to hear of them sends spirits high.

For your wonderful world we thank you oh God.
Please help us do wonderful things for you.
Just remember an old-world garden with Golden Rod
And its verdant lawns quite covered with dew.

Valerie D Maxfield-Zanetti

WAITING TO SHARE THE SUNSET

A world of transition to understand,
Alone with reflective fears.
Thoughts, a desert of endless sand
Blowing as grains of tears.

Shadows deepen around the heart
Waiting for the eclipse.
Prematurely pushed apart
As silence seals the lips.

Too late it is to say goodbye
As warm cells turn to cold.
The soul soars up as fledglings fly,
But the thread of love will hold.

Flesh and spirit finally met
But passed each other by,
Waiting to share the sunset
At their union in the sky.

Vivienne Manchester

CINDERS

The plot began to stray
When *both* my slippers
Fell away.
Down palace steps
Too steep to climb,
They crushed that pumpkin
Coach of mine.

The mice fled home
My heart grew cold,
Tears swamped that
Gown of midnight gold.

Prince Charming
Searched a million places,
Fond and in love
With other faces.

As roses have thorns
On which flesh may be broken,
So pumpkins hold seeds
Which we all might choke on.

Suzanne P Dewdney

THE HORIZON (FROM BEACHY HEAD)

From these high cliffs
On the edge of the world,
Where the vision drifts
Into nothingness, enfurled
In a haze 'twixt land and sea,
In a line at the rim of the sky
At the end of infinity
Beyond the scope of human eye,
There is a gulf between
The real and the unreal,
A void by man unseen
Which uncertain shades conceal;
For in the destiny of man 'tis writ
This gulf is crossed only by the spirit.

Roy Whitlock

A PRAYER

A nun at the chapel door
A converted oast,
No gold or silver of which to boast
With broom in hand she sweeps the floor,
A familiar sight I had seen before
Tall and thin and dark of skin,
As lithe as a deer,
Yet a woman of prayer
And when she had done,
She closed the door,
And I pondered this cameo just once more,
A lesson of life for the treasure store,
A prayer giving worth to a common chore.

Marilyn Dougan

ALEXIS

With your long dark hair
And eyes brilliant blue
Many years have passed
How I wish to find you
Your spirit runs wild
Like a fierce wind blowing
Your tears like rain
Crashing on a window pane
Your smile as happy
As the brilliant blue sky
And the shimmering green
Of springtime
Making sapphire eyes shine
Alexis where do you run?

Alexis where have you been?
When you look in the mirror
What do you see?
A dress of red velvet
Or a worn-out book?
Can you stay for a second
And take a look?
Your garden has roses
Can you smell?
Can you see the bushes
And rhododendrons as well?
One last look
And you will see
Somewhere in fading light
An image of me.

Anna Moore

A SPECIAL LADY

As a loyal nation
We readily give thanks
To a wonderful Queen Mother
Not concerned about ranks.

She talks to the children
Who lovingly present flowers,
On her own special day
In sunshine or showers.

Smiling a greeting to all whom she meets
Whether at Ascot or along crowded streets,
A Queen who has ruled with power and zest,
Dealing with a family, in ways she felt best.

A Queen who has travelled to countries afar
Welcomed by most, as their special star.
Sharing in meals, created to please,
Chatting with folk, putting them at ease.

Happy Birthday Elizabeth
Is all we can say,
To a much loved lady
On her own special day.

Rose Whiting

HURRICANE

Tall, majestic, strong they stood
deep in the dark rich earth
of many a field and wood,
where each had lived since birth.

Till with a fearful sound
a hurricane wind went by,
beating leaves to the ground,
breaking limbs with a cry.

And then, with a heavy blow,
trees that by now root-sore,
their loveliness laid low
were flung to earth's bruised floor.

Idris Woodfield

FAITH

Faith is so simple, yet so profound -
It comes from within us without a sound.
To gaze in awe at all around -
The wonders of the Lord.

Faith can move mountains - or so I am told,
It's something to nurture, something to hold.
Faith is the fence all around the fold
Of the flock of the Lord.

Faith is so powerful, it can blow my mind,
Faith is elusive, sometimes hard to find.
Faith is so loving it envelops mankind
In the spirit of the Lord.

Faith takes our problems and blows them away,
Faith sets us up for the rest of the day,
All we need to do is kneel down and pray,
To our God, the most faithful of all.

Beryl France

MY CAT

My cat's neurotic, always changing her mood,
The only thing normal is she likes the same food,
Sometimes she's calm and likes to be stroked,
Sometimes so tired as if she's been doped.
At twilight time she's off on the prowl,
She'll chase other cats and hiss and growl,
If she sees a dog she soon scampers,
And rushes home to be pampered.

A Cooper

LIFE

The meaning of life is to live,
You live your life to the full,
Live for today and not of tomorrow,
What life gives, take,
Never look but you can't change it,
Live for today,
Be the best,
If you live life, you win.

Jade Fitch

OUT OF THIS WORLD

Weightless, silent drifting
in dawn's first light,
suspended, swaying slightly
in a basket, I gained height.
Rich soil, lush grass, water
pink-tinted by the sun,
Stretched towards the horizon.
A new day had begun!

Birds wheeled, soared, floated
above the trees below.
We drift on in silence
through a world I did not know.
Beauteous isolation,
awesome tranquillity
hanging in the universe . . .
Kangaroo spotted me.
It bounced into a thicket
as flames roared into space.
God's creation was unfolding,
but no sign of human race.

Weightless, drifting downwards;
earth reached up to me -
a gentle thud, I'd landed
back in reality.

Tablelands
north of Cairns

Daphne Baker

LIFE

Life
Isn't certain. Its wishes not to be.
The feelings of despair, the pain, the anger.
Emotions mixed, feelings unbeware.
People to and fro, from each other.
Alone, sad and despair.
There is a light in the tunnel,
A glimpse of hope, a ray of sun.
People being together.
There is a bond between the people.
The strengths, and will to carry on
In a crisis or a danger.
The hopes and fears of each other.
At last the fighting is over, the ending is near.
People being united, at peace with everyone.
At last the world is together united on all fronts.
People of all creed and colour,
Forging a new beginning,
Ignoring the prejudices,
Feeling each other's pain,
Rising up against the problems
Realising that they are not alone.
But together as one, not fragmented.
Individuals . . . yes,
But also part of a larger family.
Working, living towards a common goal.
Unique as one . . . but stronger as two.

C Fenton

IT IS SPRING

Join the parade
Sing your serenade
Gone be the wintry twinge
For it is spring
A time to rejoice
Let everyone hear your voice

The winter days were forlorn
But now they are gone
The sun shines bright
The heart feels light
Put on your bonnet
And voice a sonnet

Children all joyful
Instead of tearful
Folk looking grand
As they tramp the sand
Some are for sports
Maybe the courts

Everywhere is seen a boat
Along the shore afloat
Bands playing
Children romping
Let us all sing
For it is spring

Josephine Foreman

THE MAN WITH NO NAME

With head bent low, he shuffles his feet,
In dirty old 'mac', straight off the street,
Coins put on counter, no eye contact made,
'One tea and toast with marmalade.'

Shuffling along he finds a seat,
Next to the window, overlooking the street,
Expressionless, his eyes stare straight ahead,
Waiting for his tea and hot toasted bread.

Around a steaming mug, his hands clasp tight,
Perhaps the first bit of warmth he's felt all night,
As his well-worn hands begin to thaw,
Colour in his cheeks returns once more.

Who is this man with those eyes so sad?
Many years ago, a good looking lad,
Was he a young hero who fought in the war?
First-hand devastation and cruelty saw.

Perhaps it's a loved one he once had and lost,
A business venture which failed to his cost,
Perhaps sickness and loneliness lost him friends he once had,
Now a shop doorway or barn, is his only pad.

Standing up, the old man shuffles his feet along the floor,
Puts his crocks on the counter and makes for the door,
It's cold, windy and raining, to the man all days are the same,
Down the street, a disappearing figure, the man with no name.

Veronica Tilbury

TWISTED SPIRIT

Ice in hand, fire in fist,
Faith destruction to insist,
So much defence from those who believe,
When I ask the question: Does it exist?

Love in mind, hate in heart,
Feeling lonely and always apart,
Vengeful thoughts stab my words,
Creating a world that's always dark,

Sat in the shade of the orange trees,
Debating with anger my memories,
Holding my sanity tight on me,
To stop it floating away on the breeze.

My twisted spirit fights so brave,
To save my mind becoming enslaved,
Unable to think, unable to move,
Unable to you goodbye to wave,
Unable even to dream again,
To see your image to ease my pain,

Depraved of love my heart inflicts,
Never again can I kiss your lips,
Never released to hold you close, to watch you sleep,
To bath in the liquid love that your body weeps,
Never released to share your air,
Never released from my self-created lair.

Andrew Lazarou

CONTRARY VENUS

Nothing shines quite like it up there in the sky
Like a little lantern hanging up on high
I've watched it in the twilight as it moves across the sky
No one seems to notice it with all the traffic rushing by
They say it comes from Bethlehem and called the evening star
And soon you'll see three wise men arriving from afar
For weeks I've seen this strange star come and wane
They say I'll have to wait till Christmas to see it back again
Now I've got a little secret that I can share with you
This morning I was up early when the lawn was white with frosty dew
And all the know-all parents were fast asleep in bed
Yes that bright contrary star was shining just above the garden shed
So it's no use asking grown-ups, they don't know where from when
But guess I'll keep a sharp eye out for those three wise men

Brian McDonell

ANCHOR BOOKS
SUBMISSIONS INVITED
SOMETHING FOR EVERYONE

ANCHOR BOOKS GEN - Any subject, light-hearted clean fun, nothing unprintable please.

THE OPPOSITE SEX - Have your say on the opposite gender. Do they drive you mad or can we co-exist in harmony?

THE NATURAL WORLD - Are we destroying the world around us? What should we do to preserve the beauty and the future of our planet - you decide!

All poems no longer than 30 lines.
Always welcome! No fee!
Plus cash prizes to be won!

Mark your envelope (eg *The Natural World*)
And send to:
Anchor Books
Remus House, Coltsfoot Drive
Woodston, Peterborough, PE2 9JX

**OVER £10,000 IN POETRY PRIZES
TO BE WON!**

Send an SAE for details on our New Year 2000 competition!